DEVIANTS

DEVIANTS

J L Simmons

THE GLENDESSARY PRESS — BERKELEY

Printed in the United States of America
Library of Congress Catalog Card No.: 74-91596

First printing, July 1969
Second printing, November 1970
Third printing, June 1971
Fourth printing, November 1971
Fifth printing, August 1972
Sixth printing, March 1973
Seventh printing, August 1974
Eighth printing, July 1975

This book is dedicated to the proposition that there are no "thems," there is only Us.

Grateful acknowledgment to my wife Nola and my waterbrothers Barry Winograd and George McCall for their thousand direct and subtle contributions.

Contents

DEVIANTS

THE EYES
OF THE BEHOLDER

Who's deviant?

A few years ago I carried out a small study, where I asked people to list those things or persons they regarded as deviant. There were one hundred eighty respondents, varied in age, sex, education, religion, race, and locale.

It was an interesting question because, even after a great deal of grouping and combining, the 180 subjects had called no less than two hundred and fifty-two distinct acts and persons deviant. The sheer range of responses predictably included homosexuals, prostitutes, drug addicts, radicals and criminals. But it also included liars, career women, Democrats, reckless drivers, atheists, Christians, suburbanites, the retired, young folks, card players, bearded men, artists, pacifists, priests, prudes, hippies, straights, girls who wear makeup, the President, conservatives, integrationists, executives, divorcees, perverts, motorcycle gangs, smart-alec students, know-it-all professors, modern people, and Americans.

I have informally asked the same question of many people since and have received a similar variety in response. There seems to be some agreement that some kinds of things are deviant. But this agreement is far from complete. And outside this half-consensus about a few items there is a seemingly endless variety of things which are considered deviant by at least some people.

If we went back through history and assembled together all of the people who have been condemned by their contemporaries, the range would be even greater, including the Plains Indian youth who was unable to see visions, the big-breasted Chinese girl, the early Christian skulking in the Roman catacombs, the Arab who liked alcohol instead of hashish, the Polynesian girl who didn't enjoy sex, and the medieval man who indulged himself by bathing frequently. We might soon begin to realize that virtually all of our cherished habits and values and institutions were once considered unnatural and perverse—and that most everything which may seem disgusting and abhorrent to us has been the normal, accepted way of doing things somewhere else. If we had grown up and lived in those somewhere elses, *we* would be doing those things and condemning those who didn't.

So deviance, like beauty, is in the eyes of the beholder. The fact that a small number of respondents, all drawn from one historical period and country, called so many different things deviant suggests that almost every conceivable human characteristic or activity is pariah in somebody's eyes. This means that most people (you and I included) would be labelled deviant by some existing persons and groups. Anyone who moves around much from place to place or social world to social world has probably run into this.

There is nothing inherently *deviant* in any human act; something is deviant only because some people have been successful in labelling it so. The labelling is a local matter that changes from place to place and even from time to time in the same place. To understand deviance we have to understand its environmental context. So we have to look at the people doing the labelling as much as at the deviant himself.

The wide range of opinions in our society about what is deviant has some other fascinating implications. For instance, in the very act of accepting and complying with the ideology of one social world you will often find yourself automatically violating the ideologies of other groups and persons. In just being an ordinary college student in step with his fellows, a youth will these days find himself increasingly at odds with his parents, the administration, and the townspeople where the college is located. A leather-suited black is an alien intruder in Beverly Hills, and a white in a Brooks Brothers suit is very foolish to wander alone at night in the Oakland ghettos.

If you move in several different social worlds you are likely to experience moral cross-pressures and to become of several minds in your feelings and actions. A student respondent put it nicely when we were discussing cheating and sleeping around: "I'm not sure what's right anymore so how can I say who's doing wrong?"

It might have been different in the past, but today we have many different publics, each applying a somewhat different moral standard to itself *and to everyone else.* Whatever happens—prosperity or ruin, order or disorder, suppression or rebellion—is good from some viewpoints and evil from others. With a number of different standards existing simultaneously within our current society, the definition of what is deviant has become blurred and questions of right or wrong have become hot issues for public debate—and open civil conflict.

Questions about deviance and conformity have become issues which give rise to conflict and power struggles between groups with differing standards. People begin to see themselves in camps versus other camps, wes ranged against theys. Power becomes a precious commodity as each public strives to have its thinking made into law, or at least given a legitimate place. The crucial thing about a minority, of blacks, of students, of marijuana users, of whatever, is that it has less power and is therefore often forced to live by someone else's standards (while keeping its own "quaint customs").

The crux of it is that the several publics have unequal voices in defining who is deviant and in enforcing their standards. Nor are those who have the lion's share of power to make and enforce the rules always the numerical majority. The white middle-classes around New York City make the laws and punish or reward not only themselves but also the Puerto Ricans, blacks, bohemians, and a host of other ethnic and social minorities, even though these groups outnumber the WASPS. It has, in fact, often happened that a large proportion of some populace is branded deviant by the legally constituted government. Prohibition and the current generation gap are prime examples from our own society. A change in government can mean a change in who is being investigated and a change in who is outside the law.

What does this mean? Perhaps most fundamentally that deviants have in common the antagonism of at least some powerful people in their environment. Many facts about the deviant's life and psychological makeup stem from this one shared characteristic as we will see.

People always seem to be especially fascinated with those who live beyond the conventions of society. This fascination seems to be compounded from several things. The subject serves well as a scapegoat onto which the interested person can project alienated aspects of himself or herself. There is righteous indignation toward those who violate the local taboos. Also, there is concern with the real or imagined harmful effects of deviance upon the individual and the general welfare of society. And in addition to these there is a good deal of vicarious enjoyment of the bizarre and exotic. The perennial interest in deviance can be seen by its dominance in the art, folklore, and child-rearing practices of all societies. Stories and illustrations in these areas concentrate on teaching the "right path" and depicting the evil consequences of straying from it.

Our own country and other modern nations are no exception to this preoccupation. We now have thousands of agencies staffed with hundreds of thousands of employees who spend hundreds of millions of dollars and man-hours every year attempting in some way to deal with the deviant. Parents harry their infant children to abide by our standards of right and wrong, and our mass media bombard us constantly with brackish morality plays on the same theme. Platoons of grim middle-aged women (what Philip Wylie calls the thundering third sex) run about stripping newstands, censoring movies, and even trying to foist clothing upon animals. Psychiatrists, social scientists, and journalists have carried out a legion of studies and written a whole mountain range of books and articles on delinquency, sexual perversion, crime, narcotics, adultery, marginal life, and mental illness. Deviance is probably the favorite topic of conversation among deviants themselves. And deviance is a booming business for a host of people on both sides of the law.

But how much real understanding has come out of all this attention? Do we, after all this, really know enough about the deviant to stop him or help him or even speak to him in his own language? In most respects I think the answer is no. And I think the answer is no because of some deep-rooted biases which cloud the sight of the most well-intentioned laymen and researchers who examine the deviant.

Probably the most widespread and deep-running of these biases comes from generalizing about deviants after studying that special fraction of deviants who have been caught or who have somehow volunteered for treatment, as for example, by coming to a psychiatrist or surrendering to the police. This special subgroup is most certainly unrepresentative of all deviants. In many ways these are the "flunk-outs" of the deviant world. For instance, several psychiatrists have written books about homosexuality but their facts and explanations come almost entirely from homosexuals who were so disturbed that they sought help. The less disturbed homosexuals—probably the majority—simply have gone their merry way, and remained unknown to the theorists. In like manner policemen define delinquents mostly by looking at the rebellious youths they manage to catch. And officials formulate their notions about the dangers of LSD only from the tiny fraction of users who disturb the peace or suffer gross mental disturbance.

To generalize about *all* deviants from only those who have, in some sense, failed at deviance is as one-sided and misleading as to portray school life solely on the basis of dropouts. But this is true of most present writing on deviance. Just what the differences are between those who come to the attention of authorities and those who do not will come up again and again in this book. The main point is that there is "success" and "failure" in the business of deviating from local standards, just as in every other kind of human endeavor.

Over the past dozen years as a field researcher, I have come to know hundreds of deviants of various kinds, and I've had some chance to see differences between those who got caught or went for aid and those who didn't. Most of those who got caught were patently more inept and "uncool"—either because of inexperience or because they didn't seem to care enough about themselves to take reasonable precautions. And those who went in to get help from counsellors, welfare workers, or other public officials were, on the whole, markedly more distraught and less able to cope than the rest of the deviants in their scene.

Several years ago I was in the position of knowing a dozen or so of the marijuana dealers in a large midwestern city. During the time I was in contact with this group, only two were caught and convicted by the police. And it was no surprise to anyone when each of the two was arrested because everyone in their circle had been expecting it for some time and had repeatedly warned them that they couldn't possibly go on being so careless without "getting busted." What was so surprising in that particular circle was the fact that several other careless dealers never were caught.

The other main difference between the caught and the uncaught is that many public officials are automatically more suspicious and ready to move against people belonging to minorities, the lower classes, and fringe groups such as the hippies. So it's hard to tell the real meaning of a finding that "delinquency is more common among lower class youths" or that "crime rates are higher among Negroes."

Likewise, I have been able on a number of occasions to study those who sought help from psychiatrists, social workers, or other officials. My overall impression is that most of these people would have been seeking help whether they had been deviant or not. They were the ones having the greatest problems coping with themselves and the world around them, and I suspect they resembled non-deviants who seek help more closely than other deviants who don't.

Apart from this "sampling bias" there is a further distortion. Most laymen, officials, and even scientists look upon deviants through Establishment-colored glasses. Most of the people who talk and write about deviants or who constantly deal with them in their jobs are, nevertheless, a million miles away, psychologically, from the deviant's world. The solid citizen cannot understand deviants simply because his own standards have been violated and "his" society has been affronted. And since he is usually more or less in control of the contact situation, he is in a position to make *his* perspective stick.

As all-too-human beings, most of us look upon those who don't share *our* values and aspirations as irresponsible; we see those who lack qualities we feel important as immature and poorly adjusted; and we feel that those who leave our flock are only running away from (our) reality. We view the deviant egocentrically and ethnocentrically.

This psychological and social distance is usually so vast that the official or researcher remains innocent of his subject in the same sense that a pilot may be innocent about the teeming life going on below his plane. It is true, almost by definition, that most members of a society will have little first-hand knowledge or direct experience with deviance, because if most of them did, the thing wouldn't be deviant anymore. As knowledge and experience about something spread throughout a society, the behavior or attitude moves from the parlance of "deviance" to "irregularity." This is why premarital sex is no longer considered deviant in most quarters and why the acceptance of marijuana as a mild intoxicant is becoming widespread. But as long as something remains deviant most people will know little of it, and as long as people don't know, it is likely to remain deviant.

Because of this psychological distance and innocence, people are prone to accept "common sense" pictures of deviance. And since they have little raw firsthand data to test their "reasonable" notions, the notions, true or false, become widespread and are acted upon. Many people find it reasonable to assume that peace demonstrators are Communists or dupes of Communists; that smoking marijuana is a step on the road to drug addiction; that hippies are dirty and promiscuous; that the mentally ill are dangerous to be around, and so on. But each of these assumptions is a gross oversimplification if not downright false.

The coupling of intense interest in deviance with a relative innocence about its actual substance produces a curious ariness in the voluminous writings on the subject. You often finish a book or article feeling cheated, as if the writer had only been slumming and never connected with the real live deviant.

The best glimpses might be statements made by veteran deviants themselves, and some of these are indeed excellent. But, more often than not, these statements contain the opposite biases of a person entrenched in a deviant world and innocent of many conventional social realities. To label all conventional people as plodding squares is just as simple-minded as to label all deviants sick. Also their statements are often "for the record" and are motivated by defiance or public relations persuasion so that they can't be entirely taken at face value. In addition to these problems the statements of deviants often reflect such a different way of life and way of looking at things that the ordinary person finds them hard to understand or take seriously.

Another set of biases involves faulty logic on the part of officials and laymen. The most common logical error is circular reasoning. We'll see this in many forms later, but the basic one is simple. Why does Sammy deviate? Because he's disturbed. How do you know he's disturbed? Well, just look at his deviant behavior. Needless to say, such "facts" and "explanations" go nowhere.

Another frequent logical error is reverse reasoning from consequence to premise. Almost all heroin addicts first used marijuana.

They also first breathed oxygen. Almost all call girls had early and atypical sexual experiences. They also previously learned to walk and talk. Most homosexuals report at least moderate insecurity in the presence of the opposite sex. But then so do most heterosexuals.

Another very common error is to make absolute statements about deviants on the basis of a slight statistical trend. For example, in some areas youths with delinquent records may have slightly worse school grades than youths with no records. But the generalization "delinquents are poor students" exaggerates the small differences between the two groups and obscures the far more sound generalization that there are good, average, and poor students in both groups.

All of these biases are formidable and hard to overcome. But beyond them is perhaps the most ingrained bias of all—a bias that is inherent in the very concept "deviance" itself. When you mark off an area called deviance with the intention of exploring it and explaining it, the very questions you pose are almost certain to be one-sided and unbalanced. You are almost bound to look at only one side of a two-way interrelated process, only half of the total picture. This kind of built-in one-sidedness makes objectivity virtually impossible. For example, when we define wayward youth as a problem, we only look at *our* problems with *them*, and probably never even consider *their* problems with *us*, even though this "other side" may well be the key to understanding "wayward youth."

Can these biases be overcome? More specifically, have I been able to overcome them in this book? I'm sure that I haven't, at least not entirely. But, through a series of pilot studies, field observations of several deviant subcultures and various organizations, and extended interviews with seventy deviants of various kinds and in various settings, I have tried to learn enough to look back upon society through the deviant's eyes and to appraise the public which appraises the abberrant.

Included among my respondents were political radicals of the far left and the far right, homosexuals, militant blacks, convicts and mental hospital patients, mystics, narcotic addicts, LSD and marijuana users, illicit drug dealers, delinquent boys, racially mixed couples, hippies, health-food users, and bohemian artists, and village eccentrics. I have also talked extensively with official administrators— as well as psychiatrists and social workers—and conventional people about their experiences with deviants.

The problems of gathering valid data on the feelings and daily experiences of deviants are tremendous. Unless the researcher is himself a denizen of the deviant social world, he must develop a degree of rapport and candor that is almost never achieved with the ordinary questionnaire or one-shot interview. For these reasons I adopted the informal conversation as my main "data-gathering technique." The number of such conversations per respondent varied from three to ten, and they took place in a variety of informal settings over coffee or beer, at parties, at cards, on sidewalks, in parks, on planes or buses, and so on. These conversations were "focused interviews" in that I attempted to keep the topic on deviance and to cover certain questions with all respondents. But they lacked any rigid structuring and most of the respondents seemed to feel no sense of being interviewed. If asked why I was interested in such topics, I replied simply and truthfully that I was writing a book on deviants.

Besides reporting on their own personal experiences, the respondents also served as informants about their deviant worlds. But as I've noted before, what deviants say isn't necessarily true. Even the most candid interviews can be misleading. The most valuable thing resulting from the candidness was that several of my respondents let me move for awhile with them as they moved through their own social worlds, so that I could observe first-hand what was actually going on. With the resulting added perspective, I was often able to compare what deviants said with what they did.

With the collaboration of these deviant respondents, I have tried to reduce, if not overcome, the biases discussed in the preceding pages. I have tried to neglect neither the deviant nor the society that creates him. The only request my collaborators made was that I tell it like it really is. I hope I have.

CHAPTER TWO

UNDERLYING
IMAGES

Any "theory" of deviance is much more than a set of abstract notions about its causes, nature, and consequences. It is also a *perspective* from which the phenomenon is viewed, *and this perspective itself has many consequences.* Such perspectives are usually implicit; the theorist is often not even consciously aware of them because they are so deeply buried in his general way of looking at the world. They are, nevertheless, the basis of how he feels and acts in actual situations. We can see surface reflections of such underlying perspectives when a policeman feels that wayward kids should be roughed up a little, when a psychiatrist will recommend the release of a mental patient only after he submits to degrading ward routines and parrots the doctor's diagnosis of his problems, or when a man remains silent about his colleagues' petty thieving and extramarital affairs.

These underlying perspectives or images are given expression every day in various ways: the preaching of parents, newspaper editorials and cartoons, the actions taken (or not taken) by officials, and the books and articles written by professional scientists. An image of deviance determines one's action in concrete instances. It underlies the individual's pronouncements and it even determines what he considers deviant.

Professional psychologists, sociologists, and criminologists are usually more explicit about telling the perspectives from which they are operating and, true to their scientific calling, they heroically attempt to disengage themselves from their own prejudices in their work. Most of what we know for sure about crime and deviance has come from such efforts. Because these efforts to be objective are never entirely successful, and because so much automatic credence is given those who speak in the name of Science, prejudices and value-judgments about deviance often pass as scientific fact. The ideological components buried within even the most abstract scientific theories of deviance are demonstrated, I think, by the fact that such theories can be classified as conservative or liberal, as repressive or permissive, as deterministic or free will.

Your view of deviance derives partly from your preconceptions about human nature in general (since deviants are human beings), partly from hearsay (since the vast bulk of anyone's ideas is second-hand), and partly from the nature of your own personality (since you do the labelling and reacting in concrete instances).

So both scientists and laymen approach deviants with prior images which color their attitudes and reactions somewhat independent of the deviant's actual character or behavior. The host of different perspectives in our Western civilization falls into a few broad categories.

1. **The deviant is sick.** The view of deviance as an individual pathology is one of the oldest and most widespread in Western societies, and remains the predominant perspective in psychology and psychiatry today. Within this category the explanations of why some people fail to be "decent citizens" have varied a good deal over the centuries and have included possession by devils, hereditary taint, character weakness, deliberate wilfulness, faulty physique, and mental malfunctioning. But the common denominator in all the variants is that attention focuses on the wayward individual with few if any

questions asked about the society that nurtured him. For example, when we speak about disturbed children do we examine the bleakness of the adult world they're running away from?

In the Eighteenth and Nineteenth centuries human abberrations were considered hereditary and therefore virtually beyond treatment. Deviants were simply removed from the rest of society and kept in custody (still the accepted handling of chronic schizophrenics). At the turn of this century, however, psychoanalysis—and this is perhaps its greatest contribution—succeeded in breaking through this conception of the deviant as a biological runt, and started to redefine him as a person who had simply fallen ill. This shift made the deviant at least amenable to treatment and raised some first questions about causes in the *society* for the sickness.

When the hereditary theory of deviance didn't fit, especially with minor infractions, the next explanation was wilfulness, and the most popular treatment was to break the person as if he were a wild animal. This fit in with the Judeo-Christian doctrine that people were responsible for their actions and punishable for acting wrongly (which contrasts sharply with the Islamic doctrine that disturbed people are the children of God and must be treated with reverence). Public whippings and pillories were a common sight in those days. And the chain gang is a present echo of this reasoning.

The hereditary and wilfulness variants have now faded and the view of the deviant as simply ill has become dominant. But, in the inevitable lag between professional thinking and popular opinion, those who view the deviant as ill rather than bad or genetically tainted are still regarded as liberal or even radical by many officials and laymen.

"Pathology" is invoked to explain why some members of a particular group deviate while others do not. This usually involves circular reasoning, as we have seen. People violate the norms of their group because they are psychopaths, and we know they are psychopathic because of their norm-violating behavior. Aberrant behavior is explained by internal disturbance and internal disturbance is inferred from the abberrant behavior. "Psychopath" is thus only a synonym for norm-violator, not an explanation.

Often this circularity is more subtle, the main examples being the widely used psychological tests which score the person's internal disturbance by his answers to questions about imagined behavior. The individual is presented a hypothetical situation with three "solutions" and asked which he would choose, or he is asked to make up stories about the behavior of figures in picture-cards. But such tests are indirect measures of behavior rather than measures of alleged internal states. Again, mental pathology remains only a synonym for deviance rather than an explanation of it, *because the two are not defined or measured independently of one other.*

The two can be measured independently. If a psychiatrist or official gets at least verbal expression of a person's attitudes and feelings and he can then compare these with what he actually does. Or a person can recount both his feelings and his behavior in an interview after the event.

But even when internal disturbance and external deviant behavior are separated by careful researchers and theorists, a bias discussed earlier remains—knowing only those deviants who got caught or who volunteered for treatment. If all you see are disturbed deviants, a reasonable, but actually very misleading, conclusion is that all ·deviants are disturbed.

When researchers and officials manage to overcome both of these biases there is yet another inadequacy in this perspective which is much more stubborn and difficult to eradicate—that of misplaced causation. Even if we grant that many deviants are disturbed (and many are), we cannot assume that the disturbance caused the aberration. On the contrary, we will see that most of the evidence points to the opposite assertion—that *personal disturbance is the result of societal reactions to the deviant.* For example, the mild, free-floating paranoia and defensiveness so commonly seen among pot-smokers, homosexuals, Puerto Rican gangs, and other deviant groups is easily traceable to the everpresent threat of retribution from the surrounding society, not to an earlier personality syndrome nor to anything inherent in the deviant activity itself. Looking only at the individual deviant, you can easily assume that any symptoms of internal distress must have been the original cause. And this common mistake is probably the major weakness of the view that deviants are sick.

The view is tempting because it fits so many widely held notions about human nature and the world that seem so reasonable to the conventional person. "Why else would the deviant do such crazy things?" Unable to imagine himself doing the same thing he concludes the other "must be nuts." Or he finds it necessary to sharply deny the possibility of such tendencies in himself because they would violently jar his own self-image. When Albert Reiss asked a sample of young male hustlers why they thought homosexuals sought oral-genital sex, the main response was "I don't know. I guess they're crazy." And Thomas Scheff has noted that people typically explain bizarre behavior by simply labelling it insane.

So the image prevails, and many deviants come to believe it themselves. Even when called into question, as it is more and more, a weaker, but sometimes equally insidious cousin takes its place. This is a kind of paternalism toward naughty children attitude that is developing in social welfare agencies and probation offices, a condescending attitude of "we must take care of them" much like the idea of the White Man's Burden popular in Western countries in the last century. Workers operate as unlicensed therapists applying a hodgepodge of sophomore psychology, middle-class morality, and Protestant evangelism. They demand such contrition and self-humiliation that some of their "clients" choose to do without aid or risk a prison term rather than "cooperate."

2. **The deviant is a boatrocker.** In this perspective deviance is behavior which *interferes* with the smooth running of the group, the institution, or the society. This very pragmatic perspective supports ongoing group interests—or at least the vested interests of those in power. No judgment is necessarily made about whether the deviant is sick and, indeed, there may be little or no concern about what is going on inside his head. This is the view most widely held and applied by schoolteachers, wardens, mental hospital attendants, policemen, social workers, parole officers, military officers, and others charged with keeping peace and order. This is also the orientation most emphasized by Establishment-centered theorists and researchers.

The majority of social scientists are concerned with how societies maintain their equilibrium in the face of internal and external disturbances, with the functions performed by various institutions within the System, and with how the System can attain its goals. In these concerns deviance is seen as a disturbing strain upon the well-being of the whole. Talcott Parsons, a leading social systems theorist, defines deviance as "the tendency on the part of one or more of the component actors to behave in such a way as to disturb the equilibrium of the interactive process within a given system." A host of school marms and industrial executives would echo agreement.

This boatrocking image is also implied in most psychological definitions of "normal," "adjusted," and "mature." The healthy and well-integrated person is defined as the one who happily complies with social expectations, who is a productive cog in society's machine, who wants to do what he "ought" to do.

This image has some merits. With it we can examine deviance in general, any place and any time in history. It also provides a framework for looking at stresses and mechanisms of control within any group, organization, or society. And it is superior to the individual pathology image because it explicitly considers the surrounding social environment as well as the individual and leads us to look at their complex interrelationship. For example, it makes us ask, Deviance from what?

But the approach has serious inadequacies. At first glance it appears to be unprejudiced and objective, but closer inspection reveals the heavy bias in favor of the status quo. It supports the prevailing ideology and vested interests of the group or society. "Equilibrium" is defined as maintenance and perpetuation of the existing social order.

If we support the society or group in question this image seems eminently reasonable. We agree that action must be taken against those who would screw up the works. But if we dislike the social order, we cheer the rebels on. We are pleased by youthful unrest in Communist countries but dismayed by it at home.

The boatrocking image of deviance is conservative because it claims that continuance of the existing social order is in the best interests of the entire group. But to the more disprivileged subgroups one can almost always show that a significant change in the status quo could be invigorating. For example, the existing caste system in the South benefits whites but deprives blacks and Mexican-Americans. And when you think about it, it would always be true that the status quo is most advantageous to the privileged stratum. One man's comfort can mean another man's serfdom. The enforcement of boatrocker perspective on deviance, then, favors those who would lose by change and discriminates against those who might gain from it.

A second major inadequacy is the conception of human nature and of society inherent in such an approach. The view of society as a set of interlocked parts which contribute to the functioning of the whole, populated by members so highly programmed to harmonize that we can regard them as "components," is both factually doubtful and morally questionable. Factually, this conception best fits rigid institutions such as bureaucracies and prisons, but even here it fits the official rule-book better than the actual goings on. And morally our democratic ideology asserts that societies should be made for and by the people, not the other way around.

Those in charge at every level are more or less forced to operate on the basis of this boatrocker perspective because they are expected to keep things running smoothly and quietly. Otherwise their work is called into question. University administrators, patrolmen, school-teachers, and similar public employees are in this position. Since these officials usually have more work than they can possibly do, they tend to develop a sort of callous attitude—"if you don't rock the boat, we don't much care what you do."

Some officials and writers hold a more subtle form of this view of deviance as "disturbance of the peace." They grant that a certain amount of deviation may be useful for the group as a whole by providing services which are illicit but (sadly) necessary because of imperfections in some components of the system. Thus, prostitution was tolerated within the red light district to shore up imperfections in the Victorian courtship and marriage pattern ("no sex before marriage and damn little afterwards"). Or some deviance may be permitted in order to accomplish some of the regrettably necessary "dirty work" of the system. Competent abortionists, the stool-pigeon, and a certain amount of police brutality are examples of this. But this is merely a more sophisticated version of the perspective. The "allowed" deviations are carefully kept within bounds and are still evaluated entirely from the standpoint of maintaining the existing order. They are necessary evils.

This image thus proves to be anything but neutral. Of course, a populace has some right to use this yardstick of disturbance, just as a man has some rights over what goes on in his own house. A society or group does have the prerogative of preserving order within its own province. But often this right serves as a cover for exploitation. And there is often no evidence for the claim that some type of deviance is actually disruptive.

Finally, it can be argued that some boats need and deserve to be rocked. One thinks of Nazi Germany and the Arab feudal dictator-ships; in our own society, the medieval state of mental treatment and the archaic sex laws. To say that some kinds of peace should be disturbed is a value-judgment—but so is the injunction not to disturb.

3. **Deviance is the gross violation of someone's moral standards.** We all look out upon the world from the provincial angle of our own moral standards, and our tenets of good and bad lead to moral-emotional scales for designating some people deviant. This designation always has two components: a set of moral standards and a judgment about how well someone measures up to them. And since moral standards vary from person to person, deviance is relative and subjective. Different judges may react quite differently to the same behavior.

This image is probably the oldest and most widespread of all. Everyone, square or hip, straight or criminal, is outraged by something. Because of the deep moralistic underpinnings involved, those who violate someone's standards are usually condemned fervently. Deviations become depravities, arousing the whole bag of negative reactions: indignation, disgust, revulsion, and righteous wrath. In the clamor for punishment and reprisal reason may be tossed aside. Such strong emotional feelings will often motivate people to act against a deviant even when they have no personal involvement whatsoever. This is especially likely if the deviations involve the sacred and sensitive areas of the culture. Examples are drives against pornography, public uproar against "sex offenders," drug-users, or black men involved with white girls. These "moral entrepeneurs," as Howard Becker calls them, who primly watch over the morals of others are the bane of the aberrant.

This depravity is the one held by moral and religious teachers and it is perhaps the one most widely employed by the rank-and-file populace. Although the boatrocking criterion is emphasized by officials, depravity is the mainspring of rejections and retributions on the informal personal level of daily life. At the public level it is almost routinely invoked as the ideological reason for inter-group conflicts. Ironically, it is also the perspective from which revolutionaries condemn the conditions around them. Indeed, you can look at history as the chronicle of fervently opposed moralists trying to impose their own standards upon one another.

In every society, one of the most important aims of socialization is to "program" the child's standards of right and wrong and ensure that he will always apply them to the behavior of himself and others, reacting violently against any real or suggested violation. In the long run this often creates in him an unreasoning, almost hysterical fear of deviations by others, coupled with a hysterical denial and repression of his own tendencies toward deviation. Hence, there are cases where men have beaten people to death for calling them queer, and girls have vomited at the mention of oral-genital sex. This may be one reason why society first condemns virtually anything new, from rock and roll to paperback books to psychedelics. All these reactions seem to be older than history. In *The Rise of the West* McNeill recounts how Aryan invaders in prehistoric times were so outraged by the sexual and religious practices of the flourishing Indus Valley civilization that they wiped it out in righteous wrath.

This depravity image has often crept into the social sciences disguised in technical jargon and scientific description. As a human being, a psychiatrist or a social worker is certainly entitled to his own morals. But he is not entitled to embed them "out of sight" in allegedly scientific findings and interpretations. For example, a widely used book on urban sociology describes the common sexual intimacies among engaged couples and the decline of parental authority over the life-choices of youths as a widespread breakdown in our moral fabric rather than as simply changes in behavior patterns. Likewise, the frequent assertions that those who violate social expectations are "normless" or "sociopathic" or "undersocialized" amounts to name-calling more than scientific description.

Since this image rests upon deep-seated moral premises, akin to religious convictions, it can't be criticized very effectively on logical grounds. If someone's judgment fits our own, it will seem reasonable and objective to us. The ordinary middle-class adult feels it is "natural" to define prostitution, marijuana smoking, peace demonstrations, underground newspapers, dropping out of school, occultism, and so on as aberrant. Again, only when the moral standard differs from our own can we clearly see the ethnocentric roots of this perspective.

Differences in moral standards—since they are matters of value, not fact—can only be resolved by persuasive arguments or by power struggles to see which groups force their morals into laws. I can suggest that people should be more tolerant of those who are different, or I can assert that those who righteously foist their own standards on all comers are arrogant moral imperialists. But these are personal opinions, not logical criticisms of the depravity perspective.

Subsequent chapters will show how these moral judgments actually "create" deviants, and they will show some of the consequences which follow.

4. Deviance is behavior statistically rare in a group or society. Uncommon behavior or attitudes strike most people as strange and bizarre since, by definition, rare things are little known. The unknown is regarded as dangerous until proven otherwise and, in ignorance, people often "see" whatever is strange as "evil" and "loathsome," just as a child will "see" monsters in a dark room. Eccentrics must prove themselves harmless, and even then they will be shunned and suspected by many.

In many earlier times and places, uncommonness and deviance were almost synonymous. Anything unusual was almost automatically abhorred. This rejection of anything different from the commonplace was so strong among many peoples that the term "human" was used only for members of their own tribe. All other peoples and ways of life were considered only half-human. If this seems barbaric, remember that during the Second World War Americans called the Japanese "little yellow monkeys" and, during the Korean War, called the North Koreans "gooks."

In this view "normal" becomes simply that which is statistically average. This is the basis of most psychological tests. If you fall near the average you're okay; if you fall too far from it you're not. This implies that an arithmetic average magically embodies health, well-being, and adjustment. But, as Laing and Wylie and Watts and a good many other recent writers have pointed out, when societies are "sick" and "schizophrenic" a sick "normal" person sees a healthy person as "disturbed."

Applying the statistical perspective, we would have to classify Einstein, Robert Frost, and a girl with fourteen moles on her back as deviants, along with the homosexual, the bomb-thrower, and the drug addict. So "abnormal psychology" is full of highly questionable tests and generalizations.

This perspective has now lost much of its popularity because this kind of provincialism has declined somewhat and because the equating of normal with statistical average has come under heavy attack. In our time most people have some contact with the unusual several times a day and so we've come to fear it less. Modern societies are highly mobile, and more people are more widely experienced so that fewer things are entirely unknown. But being unusual in any way is still an invitation to curiousity and suspicion. And "black power" or a "hippie invasion" can still generate mass panic.

5. **The deviant is a hero or demi-hero.** Historically this conception has been a counterpart to the sick, boatrocking, and depraved images of the deviant and it demonstrates the complexity of human reactions. Even as we put down the deviant, he sparks our desires to be free and wild, to chafe at our moral restraints. The world seems to love its outlaws even while it hangs them. For example the Spaniards have traditionally alternated between purging the gypsies and singing romantic ballads about them. Our own Western outlaws, and more recently the beats and the hippies, have produced a similar ambivalence in mainstream American society.

This image is particularly strong among the disaffected fringe who are at loggerheads with conventional society and therefore sympathetic toward its outcasts. But it is certainly not confined to them. No matter how law-abiding we are, most of us harbor a streak of lawlessness and rebellion within us. We're at least a bit reluctant about our conventionality, and who doesn't, now and then, feel some antagonism toward the forces that pressure us to conform? This is especially true if we feel the rules are largely for the convenience or benefit of others. Many members of the lower classes and of minorities feel this antagonism—and often with good reason. So many may feel a secret glee when someone robs the Bank of America or sabatoges the telephone company or runs off with a lover and thumbs his nose at the world. As long as the deviance isn't a personal risk or loss, we seem to derive some vicarious satisfaction from the rebellion and lawlessness of others. Almost none of us is so well indoctrinated with society's rules and regulations that we wholeheartedly support them. Did you ever notice that in horror movies most of the audience roots for the monsters?

From this sympathetic point of view the deviant appears sensitive and courageous. He is a semi-tragic figure who strays from the beaten path because he has been victimized by society or because he is too strong and restless to be fettered. Of course being romantic about the deviant is just as naive and misguided as being entirely outraged by him.

6. **The deviant is a human being.** Finally, there exists the image of

a person will usually have different attitudes toward different kinds of deviants; he sees the drug addict as sick, the promiscuous woman as depraved, the rowdy neighborhood youth as a disturber of the peace, his spiritualist friend as curiously different, the hobo he passes as semi-heroic, and his adulterous brother as understandably human and male.

It has perhaps become apparent by now that these various perspectives on deviance are important because they shape the societal reactions that shape the deviant.

the deviant as simply a human being like other people except that h
or she has a few quirks and some special problem making it in th
world. This image can be found in radical psychoanalytic theory an
it often contributes to the ideology of deviant groups. It also som
times arises in small towns and more stable urban neighborhood
where people come to know the local characters so well that they a
seen first as persons and only secondarily as deviants. I spent som
time in a small Midwestern town where virtually everyone knew th
one of the high school teachers was lesbian, that one of the promine
lawyers was homosexual, that one of the dentists was strung out
drugs, that one of the leading doctors sometimes performed abortior
But these people were also productive members of the communi
and well-known coffee break companions, so the townspeople tolerat
and even protected them.

People who grow up in the midst of huge metropolitan areas li
New York, Boston, and Los Angeles often know personally ma
people outside the law. They learn from first-hand experience th
Aunt Elly, the former hooker, gets corns on her feet and is good fo
strawberry soda or that Uncle Ben, who was in the numbers rac
and who killed somebody a few years back, is pretty grouchy
good protection in case of trouble. This intimacy naturally leads t
tolerance of deviants.

As a defense against the more negative images, deviants themsel
usually cling to this humane image (perhaps part semi-hero) and
frequently try to persuade their fellows and the public at large tha
is the only valid and realistic one. Prime examples of this are Dor
Corey's sophisticated arguments that homosexuality is simply
minority-group phenomenon and Ken Kesey's sensitive portrayal
the basic humanness of the inhabitants of a mental hospital in
Flew Over the Cuckoo's Nest.

An interesting variant of this image is that all human beings a
little deviant. This is a major theme in the naturalistic schools of
and literature and a common assertion in existentialist psychol
Essentially, it challenges the whole notion of a clearcut distinc
between deviant and nondeviant and, as we will see, has merit.

The perspectives sketched above are obviously not separate f
each other. They overlap and blend at many points, and most pe
think and act on the basis of several, or even all, of th
emphasizing different images in different concrete situations. Fin

CHAPTER THREE

PUBLIC

STEREOTYPING

The idea that society "creates" deviance through the same symbolic processes by which groups create "flags," "baseball," and "niggers" is hard for the ordinary person to grasp at first because these things just seem to be there in the world around him, like the rocks and trees. But there is a crucial difference between rocks and hippies. Deviants do not exist in nature, but are man-made categories. This means that deviance is not an inherent attribute of any behavior but is a social process of labelling. *Society is the creative force behind the deviant.* This doesn't mean that there is really no such thing as deviance or that the deviant is just an innocent bystander. It means that society is an active partner in producing the phenomenon called deviance and that we must look at the work of both partners if we want to understand.

This notion that we should look at least as closely at the public and officials who do the labelling and reacting as at individual deviants themselves has been gaining strength in psychiatry and the social sciences over the last few years. It had appeared earlier in the works of Durkheim and the later writings of Freud but it has only been since the Second World War that it began to gain prominence through a host of writers such as Laing, Szasz, Lemert, Erickson, Becker, Brown, and Marcuse. Kai Erickson states it concisely:

> Deviance is not a property *inherent* in certain forms of behavior; it is a property *conferred* upon these forms by the audience which directly and indirectly witnesses them. The critical variable in the study of deviance is the social audience rather than the individual person. ("Notes on the Sociology of Deviance," *Social Problems,* Spring, 1962, page 308.)

How does this "social audience" define, impute, and thereby create the deviant? How does this stereotyping process work specifically? What meaning does it have in the daily life of the deviant?

With the help of students from several classes in advanced research methods I carried out a series of pilot studies to get some of the empirical details of this process. The results of these exploratory studies provide a good deal of rather provocative data.

The pilot explorations of the public labelling process were formulated by modifying techniques social scientists use in studying attitudes toward racial and ethnic minorities.

STEREOTYPED CONCEPTIONS OF DEVIANTS

Interpreting the world around us in terms of stereotyped categories seems to be a necessary human process. How else could we organize the infinite detail and complexity of events around us into some kind of coherent order? But such categorizing is necessarily a simplification of the actual objects or events—a *selective* simplification which discards a lot of information and which may add a lot of misinformation. Stereotypes about people and things usually contain some truth. But they lead to distorted appraisals and reactions because, applied to any member individual they may impute traits which are actually imaginary and certainly ignore traits that do exist. Grouping by stereotype overestimates similarities and exaggerates differences. And finally, partly because they are self-perpetrating and self-fulfilling, stereotypes prove highly resistant to change even in the face of good contrary evidence.

Two of the pilot studies explored public stereotypes of several types of persons usually considered deviant. We hoped to define the content of public stereotypes, the extent of consensus on them, and the differences between those who rigidly stereotype and those who don't. To do this we adapted some techniques developed by Katz and Braly for exploring stereotypes of racial and ethnic groups.

We first asked eighty-nine students enrolled in a social problems class (Midwest, 1965) to answer the following question in regard to homosexuals, beatniks, adulterers, and marijuana smokers:

"**Characterize each type. What are they like and what kind of life do they lead?**"

Open-ended questions about recognizability, causes, and "what should be done about them" followed.

Over two-thirds of the students wrote a highly stereotyped portrait of every deviant type, and the responses of those who stereotyped were remarkably similar in content—almost as if they were all echoing the same packaged images. The only striking differences among the students showed that some stereotyped and some didn't. This seemed to be something of a natural dichotomy. The stereotypers portrayed the deviants as dark, haunted creatures skulking beyond the pale of ordinary life; the others described deviants as just people who happened to have a few different habits. An illustration of the first group is the following description of the marijuana smoker by a male sociology major.

> . . . a greasy **Puerto Rican boy** or the shaky little **skid row bum.** As for the life led, it is shiftless, unhappy, **dog eat dog for survival.** I guess marijuana is used as a means of avoiding reality. The pleasure that comes from the drug outweighs the pleasure of life as it really is.

The following portrayal of homosexuals by a female sophomore illustrates the nonstereotyped responses.

> As far as I know the homosexual is not like anything. They are merely people who have different ideas about sex than I do. They probably lead lives which are normal and are different only in the way they receive sexual gratification. They have no distinguishing characteristics.

Emotional reactions toward the deviants ranged from revulsion to pity to contempt among the stereotypers, and from mild sympathy to no apparent reaction among the nonstereotypers. The only exceptions were in the attitudes toward beatniks—a moderate fraction of both groups mingled disapproval and admiration.

From these open-ended responses we constructed a second questionnaire which listed 70 traits extracted by content analysis. The list included a variety of positive, negative, and neutral traits from which a new sample of respondents could choose in building their portraits.

The questionnaire was given to a sample of 134 adults selected on the basis of a quota sampling formula designed to guarantee wide variation in age, education, sex, region, and race. From the list, respondents selected traits they considered characteristic of marijuana smokers, adulterers, homosexuals, beatniks, and political radicals. They were encouraged to add any words they considered important (but almost none did so). Then they were to go back and circle those five words they considered most important for describing each group. Our analysis showed that these circled words reliably represented a respondent's entire list and these key words are the basis for the following tables.

Table 1 presents the most frequently chosen traits, along with the percentage of respondents circling them, for each of the five deviant types. For each deviant type, a handful of traits accounts for a large proportion of the responses and many traits were ignored or chosen only once or twice. Thus this multiple questionnaire matched the open-ended one in showing a fairly high degree of stereotyping.

The stereotype differs for each deviant type. The marijuana smoker is seen as an insecure escapist, lacking self-control and looking for kicks; the beatnik is a sloppy, immature nonconformist; the adulterer is immoral, promiscuous, and insecure; the homosexual is perverted and mentally ill; the political radical comes off as ambitious, aggressive, and dangerous. All but the radicals were described as lonely and frustrated, but only one trait regularly characterized all five types—irresponsible.

The composite word portraits drawn by the respondents are almost wholeheartedly negative for the marijuana smoker, homosexual, and adulterer—the only real difference of opinions being whether they should be pitied or condemned. Beatniks and political radicals were regarded a bit more equivocally, even respectfully, though clearly off the beaten path. Words defining the beatnik image included artistic, imaginative, and happy-go-lucky, and radicals were

TABLE 1

Traits Encircled as Descriptively Most Important
For Each of the Five Deviant Groups
N = 134

Marijuana smokers	%	Beatniks	%	Adulterers	%	Homosexuals	%	Political Radicals	%
Looking for kicks	59	Sloppy	57	Immoral	41	Sexually abnormal	72	Ambitious	61
Escapist	52	Non-conformist	46	Promiscuous	36	Perverted	52	Aggressive	47
Insecure	49	Escapist	32	Insecure	34	Mentally Ill	40	Stubborn	32
Lacking self-control	41	Immature	28	Lonely	32	Maladjusted	40	Non-conformist	32
Frustrated	34	Individualistic	27	Sinful	31	Effeminate	29	Impulsive	28
Excitement seeking	29	Lazy	27	Self-interested	29	Lonely	22	Dangerous	28
Nervous	26	Insecure	26	Lacking self-control	28	Insecure	21	Individualistic	26
Maladjusted	24	Irresponsible	24	Passionate	24	Immoral	16	Self-interested	23
Lonely	22	Self-interested	20	Irresponsible	22	Repulsive	14	Intelligent	22
Immature	21	False lives	18	Frustrated	21	Frustrated	14	Irresponsible	21
Weakminded	17	Artistic	16	Immature	16	Weakminded	12	Conceited	15
Irresponsible	15	Maladjusted	16	Sensual	16	Lacking self-control	12	Imaginative	14
Mentally Ill	13	Harmless	14	Over-sexed	14	Sensual	11	Excitement-seeking	9
Pleasure-loving	11	Imaginative	13	Sexually abnormal	13	Secretive	11		
Dangerous	11	Lonely	12	Pleasure-loving	12	Over-sexed	10		
		Imitative	11	False lives	11	Dangerous	10		
		Frustrated	10	Maladjusted	11	Sinful	10		
		Happy-go-lucky	9			Sensitive	10		

imaginative and intelligent. Both beatnik and radical were also credited with individualism by over one-fourth of the respondents. The predominant pariah image of both types, however, remained only attenuated by the positive and neutral imputations.

In summary, the data from this second pilot study supports the contention that discernible stereotypes of at least some types of deviants do exist in our society, and the content of these images is fairly consistent. Their crucial importance for the deviant will be taken up shortly.

As we found with the open-ended study, the respondents in this pilot study seemed to fall into something of a natural dichotomy of high and low stereotypes. We sorted respondents into these groups by comparing their circled words to the lists in Table 1. We then looked for other differences between the two groups.

We first wanted to see whether the tendency to stereotype was a "personality trait" of individuals. Do those who stereotype one kind of deviant tend to stereotype all types? To check this we computed the degree of association between the scores on every pairing of the five deviant types. All ten of the resulting associations were statistically significant beyond the .001 level. The correlations ranged from .80 to .22, and eight of the ten were above .50, suggesting strongly that the tendency to stereotype deviants is a general characteristic of the appraiser himself.

We also found a marked relationship between educational level and the tendency to stereotype deviants. Comparing the dichotomy to amount of education (some schooling, high school graduation, at least some college) showed strong relationships (gamma ranging from .64 to .38; for the totalled stereotype scores, the relationship with education was .63). As a reliability check we intuitively sorted the respondents into high or low stereotypers and the association between this intuitive sorting and education was even stronger (.75). So the evidence suggests a marked tendency for stereotyped thinking to be associated with lack of education.

But this finding can't be taken at face value. For one thing the associations were largely one-way. The majority among even the most highly educated group applied unequivocally negative stereotypes to most or all the deviants included. The associations actually rested on the fact that *none* of those low in education was a stereotyper. The "success" of education in teaching more thoughtfulness in appraising people is therefore relatively small.

In the second place, the more educated groups expressed what we might call "secondary stereotypes" of the deviants, evidently derived from psychiatric explanations of human behavior so fashionable in high- and middle-brow mass media. These images are more enlightened than the traditional stereotypes and I will grant that psychoanalytic pity is a softer stance than rigid rejection. But a close reading of the responses themselves suggests that many of the educated are merely more subtle in their stereotyping.

We also found a fairly strong inverse relationship between stereotyping and a composite liberalism measure which included items about politics, economics, international affairs, sex, divorce, child rearing and religion. The relationship (gamma) between liberalism and tendency to stereotype was negative .57. The individual questionnaires showed that this finding was reliable; compared to moderates, liberals stereotyped less and conservatives stereotyped more. Since liberalism involves broadmindedness and a softening of preconceptions this finding is not surprising.

We were also able to directly compare tendencies to stereotype with intolerance or social distance (the degree of intimacy which one person allows another) for two deviant groups, the homosexual and the adulterer. The relationship (gamma) between expressed intolerance and the tendency to stereotype the homosexual was .70 and for the adulterer was .67.

INTOLERANCE TOWARD DEVIANTS

The third pilot study explored the amount of public intolerance toward various kinds of deviants and sought other variables related to this intolerance. Again we followed the lead of the many studies which have been conducted on racial and ethnic discrimination.

A questionnaire was developed which measured the degree of social distance between the respondent and members of five ethnic groups (Germans, Mexicans, Negroes, Chinese, Jews) and thirteen deviant or semi-deviant groups (alcoholics, prostitutes, lesbians, political radicals, marijuana smokers, ex-mental patients, homosexuals, atheists, ex-convicts, intellectuals, adulterers, beatniks, and gamblers). For each of these groups the respondent could choose from seven answers ranged in increasing degree of rejection:

1. Might marry or accept as a close relative.
2. Might have as a close friend.
3. Would accept as a next door neighbor.
4. Would accept in my school, church, and so on.
5. Would accept in my community, but would have no contact.
6. Would accept as resident of my country but not my community.
7. Would not accept at all, even as a resident in my country.

The questionnaire, after pretesting, was administered to two hundred and eighty respondents, again selected with a quota sample formula to produce diversity in age, sex, race, education, and region of the country. The questionnaire included a variety of other measures which we'll turn to shortly.

By now the main finding should come as no surprise. We found a high relationship (gamma of .78) between the summed scores of intolerance toward the deviant groups and intolerance toward ethnic minorities. The intercorrelations among all the pairings of the individual groups were also quite high (ranging from .91 to .44). Those who rejected Mexicans tended to reject intellectuals, those who were tolerant of Negroes were tolerant of homosexuals, those who would have no contact with ex-mental patients also wanted no contact with Jews, and so on. This means that the tendency to accept or to discriminate against those who differ seems to be a basic part of a person's way of looking at the world. If a new fringe group comes along next year, people who now reject hippies and Negroes will rail against the newcomers. And those who give the Mexican laborer and the homosexual a fair hearing will look at any new group before they leap to condemn.

The average social distances toward the thirteen deviant groups appear in order of increasing rejection in Table 2. These averages can't be taken too seriously because the sample was not representative and the data were gathered in 1965, a long time ago in our swift-changing times. For example, perhaps the homosexual is now a bit more acceptable and the political radical a good deal less. Relationships between measures are far more reliable than such averages. An even greater bias is that people often verbally express more tolerance and acceptance of others than they actually practice. So we can safely assume that the American populace is, in fact, more intolerant than these averages. But the scarcity of data on public attitudes toward deviants requires us to make do.

TABLE 2
Average Social Distance Toward Various Deviant Groups

Groups (In Order of Increasing Intolerance)	Mean Social Distance (Range 1 to 7)
Intellectuals	2.0
Ex-mental patients	2.9
Atheists	3.4
Ex-convicts	3.5
Gamblers	3.6
Beatniks	3.9
Alcoholics	4.0
Adulterers	4.1
Political Radicals	4.3
Marijuana Smokers	4.9
Prostitutes	5.0
Lesbians	5.2
Homosexuals	5.3

It is heartening to see that ex-mental patients and ex-convicts (who certainly have enough problems on their own) are not too strongly rejected by the respondents, although other studies have shown that they are, in fact, often discriminated against in job, family, housing, and so on. But disheartening is the degree to which sexual deviants (adulterers, homosexuals, and prostitutes) are so roundly repudiated. It is also interesting that alcoholics are far more acceptable than marijuana smokers, although all the medical evidence indicates that the former are far more dangerous and costly to society.

Respondents over forty years old were significantly less tolerant of every deviant (and every ethnic) group. Likewise, the least educated expressed the most social distance. The overall relationship between amount of education and intolerance toward the deviant groups was negative .45. The sexes differed significantly in attitudes toward only three of the deviant groups; women were significantly more intolerant of prostitutes and lesbians, and men were more intolerant of male homosexuals. Women may find prostitutes and lesbians personally threatening, while men may be threatened by the male homosexual, but this is only speculation.

We asked the respondents "what should be done" with six of the deviant groups (marijuana smokers, adulterers, homosexuals, beatniks, prostitutes, and radicals) and gave them a choice of six answers ranging from "nothing" through "they should be forced to accept help from officials..." to "prison is too good for them; they should be publicly whipped or worse." Reactions were mild only for the adulterer and the beatnik; stronger measures were recommended by the majority for the other groups. The correlation (gamma) between total social distance scores and total "what should be done" scores was .69. The intolerant wanted society to take strong action. The educated, the young, and those scoring high on the composite liberalism scale were significantly milder in their recommendations. (The subgroup differences were significant far beyond the .001 level.) The relationship between social distance and the liberalism measure was also moderately high (.51).

We asked the respondents to say whether heredity, psychological disturbance, or social conditions caused the deviant behavior in these six groups. The majority thought psychological factors were to blame for beatniks, adulterers, pot smokers, and prostitutes, but felt homosexuality was biological and radicalism stemmed from social conditions. More older people applied "heredity" to all six groups, while the young, the educated, and the liberal more frequently blamed social conditions for all six types.

We asked the respondents how much personal contact they had had with the same six groups of deviants used in the last two questions. The majority admitted little contact with any of them. Either they met such people only casually or heard of them from others, although a moderate fraction said such people had been acquaintances of theirs. Men and liberals reported far more contact than women and conservatives. The relationship (gamma) between intolerance and lack of contact was .55 and those with less contact called for stronger action in answer to "what should be done?"

Finally, we asked the respondents specific questions about their attitudes toward deviants. The overwhelming majority said breaking the law was never permissible, "once a criminal, always a criminal," and penalties should be stiffer. But the majority also said if they saw someone using dope they probably wouldn't turn him in, and if they discovered that a friend was homosexual they probably wouldn't break off the friendship.

In summary, the major conclusion from the pilot studies is that most people don't like deviants very much. But this generality is itself a stereotype because there were great variations in the responses to every item in each of the studies. The range of views means that we can't speak of *the public* as if views of pacifists or drug users or anything connected with deviants were universal. The fact that there is a range of public attitudes is as important as the fact that some agreement exists.

Even an individual is seldom singleminded. Interviews and individual questionnaires revealed equivocation and self-doubt even in the staunchest bigots. And even the typical respondent's predominantly negative stereotypes almost always included a smattering of counter-opinions and qualifications. "Other opinions" are crucial, we will see.

SOME CONSEQUENCES OF THE STEREOTYPES

We've seen that public stereotypes of many different kinds of deviants do indeed exist. But this finding is of little or no importance unless the stereotypes affect deviants themselves and our society at large. Do such effects exist?

In the first place we shouldn't overlook the fact that these stereotypes sometimes provide useful information when people interact with deviants. They are distortions and oversimplifications but still may have some *descriptive validity*. They thus serve as do so many other generalities about the world ("don't ride your bike in the street," "older people are more conservative," and so on). It would seem that they do contain some truth because, with their help, the populace does better than chance in recognizing deviants and predicting their behavior.

Robert Merton and others have shown, however, that even those aspects of the stereotype which happen to be "true" may only be the self-fulfilling result of applying the stereotype in the first place. Take, as an example, a man who goes to a prostitute with the image in his mind of her as a dispicable creature unfit for regular human society, an object fit only for servicing his sexual lusts. As he walks into her room his image is bound to be reflected in his face and his actions.

In reply, the girl is not likely to be a very warm, responsive sex partner. She may haggle over the price and barely conceal her distaste. The man leaves with his stereotype confirmed. Or a cop who believes that Puerto Rican kids are vicious roughs up every one he finds involved in petty offenses. As time passes he points out the growing viciousness of gang activities on his beat to his superior, as hard evidence that Puerto Ricans are vicious and thus need rough handling. His superior is absolutely convinced when a vicious Puerto Rican kid eventually kills the cop.

Second, as Howard Becker has shown, these negative stereotypes are perhaps the most effective measure societies have for curbing deviance. Surrounded by these baleful images as we grow up most of us reject deviance or even refuse to contemplate it. Unless a person is acting out self-hatred this negative image must be neutralized before an individual will, for example, become a marijuana smoker. And in an open-ended questionnaire, three-fourths of an advanced sociology class in a major midwestern university (spring of 1965) characterized the pot smoker as physiologically enslaved by the drug, although even the Federal Narcotics Bureau admits it is nonaddictive. So this control mechanism works.

A third effect of these stereotypes is that they result in virtually automatic rejection and isolation of those who are wrongly or rightly labelled deviant. They are prejudged and largely helpless to alter their evaluation and treatment by others. The force of such negative images is not necessarily diminished even when a person becomes aware that he is stereotyping, as one respondent explained:

> **I realize that this is a stereotypical picture, but nevertheless it is my conception. For me homosexuality is repulsive. It is inconceivable to me how anyone can physically love someone of the same sex.**

These negative stereotypes may imprison the deviant in his deviant role. This deviant role imprisonment occurs because the stereotype leads to restricted opportunities. The most notable examples are cases where a police or mental hospital record impedes a person's chance of going straight and leading an ordinary life. Ironically and tragically many people return to jail or to the mental hospital because no other paths were open to them.

We must realize that such rejection of deviants may be realistic in terms of the self-interests of those reacting. Even the enlightened reformer is being realistic when he hesitates to let his children become involved with delinquent or drug-using youths. And we can't entirely damn a businessman for hesitating to hire an ex-mental patient with a spotty work history for an important deadline job. Nevertheless the sum of these personal decisions—many of them made by liberal and kindhearted people—makes it especially difficult for someone labelled deviant to make it in conventional society.

There is yet another unpleasant consequence of these negative stereotypes. From among those who come to the attention of teachers, the police, or other officials by breaking the rules, the stereotypes select the ones to be labelled "deviant." Studies have shown that though a sizeable proportion of people have committed deviant acts at one time or another in their lives only a few ever get labelled deviant. Among those who commit deviant acts, the ones who possess additional qualities which concur with the stereotype are far more likely to be labelled and processed "deviant."

Having some of the stereotypical traits of a deviant increases the likelihood of being so labelled. Conversely, if you deviate but don't fit the stereotype you may escape detection; and even if you are caught, you are likely to be let off lightly. For example, cops are far more likely to stop hippy-looking drivers and search for illicit drugs, and effeminate men must constantly face the suspicion that they are queer. Again, there may be some varying degree of truth in the assumed connection; long-haired drivers may indeed be more likely to be carrying drugs, for instance. And further truth accrues through self-fulfilling processes as we've seen; if you're treated as a homosexual or a dangerous radical, you're more likely to become one.

Such visible attributes as effeminacy, long hair, or a vacuous look in the eyes, which are facets of public stereotypes, are, in fact, used extensively by police and other officials as a kind of "first screening" of the people in their domain. If any social turbulence has arisen, those possessing such visible traits fall, rightly or wrongly, under immediate suspicion.

The "cool" deviant knows this full well and will often strive to develop a conventional facade in public. He will, in effect, learn to *impersonate* conventional people in his looks and actions in order to escape attention. Some deviants even get a sort of sour pleasure out of passing for straight.

Many "findings" in scientific studies of deviants are artificial results of these public stereotypes. For example, the widespread belief that delinquents come from broken homes creates its own confirming evidence. Policemen warn middle-class kids from solid homes and arrest lower-class punks for the same offense. And the courts usually dismiss children to their parents if the home is intact, sentence them to juvenile authority if the home is disrupted. It has been shown statistically that, for the same offenses, minority group members, lower class persons, and those who display "fringie" characteristics are more likely to be arrested, more likely to be convicted, and less likely to be paroled.

One other use of these stereotypes is a sort of reversal. In anger or condemnation people often pin deviant tags on one another even though all parties know they have no validity. Many slang epithets such as punk (the passive partner in anal intercourse), jerk (autoerotic male voyeuer) and brown-noser (analinguist) have gained wide popularity this way. It's perhaps significant that in an argument, when all logic and persuasion fail, people resort to calling each other deviant.

These are some of the processes through which public stereotypes get translated into concrete actions that affect deviants. But what are the deviants' attitudes toward the public?

What are your feelings toward those who reject and condemn you? Complicated, probably, but certainly not warm and pleasant. Likewise the deviant becomes angry and alienated by public persecution. Society and the deviant thus become partners in a vicious game of mutual estrangement, aggression, and degradation.

CHAPTER FOUR

SIMILARITIES

AND DIFFERENCES

Let's start with the deceptively simple assertion that deviants belong to the human species. This means that we can apply what is known about human beings in general to the special case of deviant human beings. This application forms a classic syllogism:

All human beings possess characteristics a,b,c, . . . x

All deviants are human beings.

Hence, all deviants have characteristics a,b,c, . . . x

Deviants, like other humans, have hopes and aspirations, fears and insecurities, habits and daydreams. They worry about their appearance, have to go to the bathroom, like coffee in the morning, get headaches, and have corns on their feet. And they have their side of the story—their version of reality. These facts are often lost sight of in the hot pursuit of justice and revenge, when the deviant becomes a faceless object to be dealt with like a wartime enemy. Once, after having a panel discussion involving several ex-convicts, a girl came up to me and said, "It never occurred to me before that deviants buy shoes like me."

People learn to be deviant in essentially the same way they learn to be businessmen or housewives or successful students. Most deviant behaviors and attitudes are learned from mothers (like arithmetic or kissing), not invented by the individual on his own. David Matza has pointed out how our society has always had subterranean counter-traditions. Even the most conventional members of society learn at least something of these counter-traditions in the process of growing up. We all know a little about the rogue, the gypsy, the bohemian, the mystic. From books and magazines and television we all learn some of the do's and don't's of being a successful reprobate. As the differential association theorists have pointed out, all members of our society incorporate both conventional and deviant attitudes, but the relative weighting of these varies from person to person. Even the conventional hold some deviant beliefs, while even the most deviant have internalized many conventional attitudes. Their reversed positions are actually mirror images, and this reversal has many implications.

Deviant behavior, like all human activity, takes its shape largely under social pressures. Since the *violation* of expectations is the point of issue, this fact is usually lost sight of. But there are three special senses in which deviants conform to these pressures. In the first place all deviants are conventional in the vast majority of their beliefs, attitudes, and activities. Even the most unconventional denizens of our society, for instance, prefer ground beef to rotted camel meat, speak a language which is unmistakably a mid-century American dialect of English, drive on the right-hand side of the road, and take aspirin for a headache. The vast bulk of a deviant's characteristics will be statistically common and morally accepted. Our upbringing in the same historical place and time gives us all—deviant and straight—a thousand common bonds.

Secondly, deviants do comply with the norms and practices of their groups or the groups they aspire to join. A person often deviates from the society at large just by going along with his crowd. This compliance is partly to confirm one's membership and allegience, but it isn't altogether voluntary. In deviant subcultures you will usually find a good deal of in-group pressure upon the members to comply with group standards.

Finally, deviants to some extent fulfill the negative public stereotypes of them, as we have seen in Chapter Three. A person who strays beyond conventionality retains emotional ties with society's stereotypes. These ties sometimes make it hard for the deviant to accept his own behavior. Prostitutes become disgusted with themselves, homosexuals believe they are emotionally disturbed, drug addicts are convinced they lack the willpower to stop. Further, the rank and file of society, by using their stereotypes, often force the deviant to react in a manner that fulfills them.

Like all other human beings, deviants must also maintain themselves physically, psychologically, and socially. They must solve the problems of procuring goods and services, they must manage their interpersonal affairs, and they must maintain themselves psychologically.

Although these existential problems face all other human beings, they are compounded for the deviant by public disapproval, or potential disapproval of this deviance. Societies help those who play by the rules and punish those who don't.

On the whole, societies facilitate the procuring of morally acceptable goods and services and frustrate the procuring of taboo ones. Such restrictions are not entirely successful, partly because deviants aren't as bound by the rules. But the restrictive efforts of straight society are incessant and diverse. It's much easier to get liquor than marijuana. Married couples can rent apartments and have babies far more easily than couples simply living together. It's easier and safer for a guy to try picking up a girl than another boy. Ivy League types get more job offers and scholarship loans than students with long hair and sandals. And so on. A superintendant of schools in Iowa told me he had the doors removed from the bathroom stalls so students wouldn't masturbate during school hours.

Our point of view shapes our attitude. To a deviant, deviance can be entirely reasonable and rational. From where he sits, with his needs and attitudes, and the situation as he perceives it, what he does is logical. We may say that the paranoid is unreasonable to assume that the world is against him, but we wouldn't say that his actions are unreasonable if that assumption were true. So the conventional person differs from the deviant fundamentally not only in tastes but in assumptions about reality. The conventional person, puzzled and fearful of the deviant, dismisses him as irrational without considering the deviant's beliefs and fulfillments. For example, Albert Cohen has shown how delinquent boys carry out vandalism simply to gain prestige from their cronies, their way of "getting ahead in the world." Lemert, Laing, and many others have documented the fact that there is always some factual basis to the seemingly deranged contentions of even the most out-and-out psychotics. And when I was an undergraduate in psychology a sign on the department bulletin board gave everyone pause:

DO YOU FEEL LIKE THE WORLD
IS PLOTTING AGAINST YOU?

WELL IT IS.

We can't just say that deviance is the violation of institutionalized rules and expectations by a small minority of psychological freaks. The majority diverge to some extent from the laws and mores of every society and every organization. If you've never hedged a little on your income tax or done a bit of petty thieving or had a secret sexual adventure, you're either a rare and saintly person or you've lived an incredibly quiet life. Some divergence is often tolerated and sometimes even encouraged. Also, most organizations and societies have a number of sub-groups struggling with one another because their aims and standards and views conflict. The idea that deviants are a different species of men and women ranged against a vast majority of upright citizens falls apart under closer inspection.

Everyone deviates to some extent from the highest moral standards of their society. "Deviance" really boils down to a matter of degree. Neither of the two imaginable extremes of behavior in any group—complete conformity or total disregard of all standards—is actually possible.

Complete conformity is impossible for a variety of reasons. In the first place most moral standards are not altogether realistic; they are high ideals, difficult to keep amid the temptations of daily life. Complete and consistent morality is a luxury few organizations or persons feel they can afford and still be effective. Also, most norms are rather abstract and categorical, hard to apply in specific situations, especially when conditions change. In civil wars and revolutions, for instance, both sides often claim to be fighting for the very same ideals. Finally, the various rules and ideals of a group or society may be inconsistent with one another; sometimes you have to betray either the law or a friend, your commanding officer or your own conscience. Real life has more moral dilemmas than fiction.

If no one obeyed the rules there would be literally no dependability or predictability or coherence to anyone's actions. There would be no mutual understandings, and experience would be of no value in human affairs. It would be worthless as a guide because such random behavior is physically impossible for any living organism. Even the tropisms of one-celled life-forms are generalized responses applied to specific situations. There is no record of human beings surviving in such a chaotic state. Julian Steward and George Homans have shown that even under conditions of disaster or nearly complete social disruption and collapse, social life falls apart only down to the small group level, never to the level of everyone alone and on his own. If anyone independently even begins to be unpredictably random in his behavior, he wreaks such social havoc that he is summarily dealt with by the people around him. Among the Eskimos, if a man became troublesome by disregarding all conventions, several other men would get together and kill him.

It seems, then, that every person falls somewhere between these two imaginable extremes in his behavior, bending the rules to meet desires and circumstances but never entirely ignoring them. Along with the high ideals of a society or group is always a range or band of more or less acceptable divergences. Beyond this range of more or less tolerated behaviors there will be limits past which it is deemed unacceptable to go. Arguments about proper conduct will usually pertain to the accepted range—even the opponents agree against "going too far." For instance, a teacher is free to dress as he likes only within limits. There's the mild expectation that his choice include a tie and jacket; there's a rather strong sentiment against conducting classes in a knit shirt and shorts; the school might dismiss anyone lecturing in his pajamas; and things would get sticky indeed if the instructor appeared in the raw. In the area of religion, it is difficult to become a deviate in our own society as long as you stay within the broad range of Judeo-Christian alternatives. But a witch or a Stonehenge Druid would have his troubles. In American politics the band of acceptable alternatives is much narrower—you're either Democrat, Republican, or out of it. In every area of human activity in every group, freedom is only within such limits.

As the actual practices of the people living in a society always more or less diverge from that society's official rules and ideals, the brunt of social pressure is not to make everyone adhere strictly to these rules and ideals but to keep the divergences within certain bounds. *The rules are to be bent but not broken.* The prevailing practices in a society are the divergences most common and most acceptable. Deviance is simply divergence that is much greater than the divergence of the majority, or at least the majority of the groups and classes in power.

By allowing divergences and lapses, the effective majority tempers idealism with realism. Everybody has desires and aspirations as well as morals and ideals, and when a person's "shoulds" and "wants" are in conflict, his temptation is to hedge a little on the "should." To the extent that the moral structure frustrates widespread desires, there will be widespread compromising. And such compromises may become so widespread that they become the new moral standard. This seems to be happening with the rise of a new sexual morality in our time.

In growing up we learn the actual practices of our society along with the ideals and rules. Although there is some effort to hide "the realities" from children, we still "lose our innocence." Among other things, some guilt develops from the fact that few of us come very close to living up to the ideals we learn and espouse.

These prevailing practices make up the "informal culture" which is as basic a part of every group as the formal structure—and frequently more important in daily life. The young or the new recruit reaches full status only when he "learns the ropes," when he becomes conversant with the realities as well as the ideals. He finds there is often more social pressure on him to conform to the prevailing divergences than to the official ideals.

The prevailing practices tend to be more realistic about human emotions and more in tune with current realities than the official ideals and rules. The ideals change slowly because they reflect accumulated behavior habits. When societies undergo rapid social change, as ours now is, the laws and the moral structure lag behind the current practices. Groups with a new morality based on new behavior habits arise to engage in ideological warfare with the "old guard." Our present generational conflict is a clear example of this.

Of course, deviations from the official rules and ideals don't always involve just opportunism or human frailty. The man not in step with his fellows is often marching to a different drummer. There are few, if any, scenes today where the participants all agree on a single moral standard, *and the deviant often turn out to be supporters of a different camp.*

All evidence from the social sciences suggests that the more dissimilar a person's attitudes from others the more intolerant he'll be. But most of us have learned more than one standard and feel some antagonism toward the rules that constrain us, so this intolerance is not singleminded. We find a good deal of ambivalence all along the spectrum of divergence from the high ideals.

The admiration which most of a society or group feels for its own idealists is nonetheless tinged with a certain amount of indignation and contempt. Idealists make the rank-and-file at least a little uncomfortable and defensive about their own behavior. The homage paid them is usually from a distance because they are also regarded as a little stuffy and straight-laced, perhaps a bit strange (maybe even deviant). Those who follow the prevailing divergences are regarded as slothful by the idealists and as timid sheep or self-righteous hypocrites by the deviants. And the deviants are condemned, but also admired and envied a little.

This ambivalence affects everyone along the line of divergence. The idealists find that they are mocked and subverted as well as listened to; and they are sometimes even the target for the release of pent-up violence during social upheavals. Those who engage in the prevailing divergences—the rule-bendings—are never entirely safe from the possibility of being punished for doing no more than what most other people are doing. For instance, there are college youths now serving long prison sentences for smoking one marijuana cigarette. It's ironic that the most inexperienced are most likely to become such "social casualties." And the ambivalence all along the line means that there is a good deal of covert support for such activities. Without such widespread tacit support (which includes support by lack of opposition) widespread deviance would be impossible.

When someone diverges moderately from the effective majority, his deviations are usually tolerated while efforts are made to bring him back into the fold. But when the deviations become more than moderate, the majority's ambivalence is resolved and the ambiguities cleared up by labeling the person "deviant" or "crazy." Mental illness is a prime example of differences singled out and exaggerated by a label that the "nut" is more or less forced to accept. All of the basic similarities between "the disturbed" and "the normals" are glossed over, and the power of the state forces the disturbed to occupy a special category stripped of most rights of a citizen. Society is then free to do virtually whatever it wants with his property, social assets, body, and mind.

The young man in the following case is certainly disturbed, but no more so than most people at one time or another. (This case was gathered by Jennifer Gibbs.)

George is twenty-four, white, middle-class. He has been in a large state mental hospital now for thirteen months classified as "schizophrenic—undifferentiated type," the residual category in the hospital's classification system. Here's his story.

"When I graduated from high school I had a big choice: to go to work or go to college. I couldn't see a clear path for myself so it didn't seem to matter much to me what I did, but I went to college anyway because that's what my mother wanted me to do. I didn't do very well though. One day a professor asked me why I was going to school if I didn't like it. That started me thinking about a whole lot of things because I didn't know I didn't like school. But he was right; I didn't like it at all—it was so phony. All the people were phony. Nobody was friendly to me either. I had a girl and she told me how beautiful the world was, how beautiful people were and how great it was to be alive. But I looked around and I didn't see that at all. I told her she was wrong, that these were a bunch of 'hollow men, stuffed men' (I remember, I read about them in a poem). She got angry and said that she would never see me again. But she was as phony as the rest of them. Still, I believed that somewhere I could find people that understood what I meant, that weren't so phony. School was not the place for me.

"My parents were upset when I quit, so I came to California. They couldn't understand what I was saying about phony people. I thought California would be different, and besides, my parents didn't want me back. They only cared for me if I was 'their' son and did what they wanted. I didn't know what I had done that was so wrong. I was beginning to get confused about my life and other peoples' lives. There were so many contradictions in what they said and what they did. My parents said they loved me yet they made me leave.

"I had a little money but I needed a job so I went to Los Angeles. I was a pretty good draftsman but no one would hire me for that without my degree, so I finally got a job working at a warehouse. I didn't mind the work for a while but later it started to get to me. I started to wonder if I'd be working in a warehouse all my life. Maybe I should go back to college. But I couldn't admit to my parents that I'd made the wrong decision. The world seemed a terribly grim place; I could push boxes around all day or I could get an education and do something else. But I didn't know what I would do after college and I didn't want to go back to all those phony people (although I don't know why; they were the same in L. A.). I was beginning to feel trapped.

"I went down to the docks a lot of the time after work and would look at the ships and wonder where they were going. I wanted to go far away from L. A., the country, and my parents. I met a girl through one of the guys at the warehouse and began dating her. She was all right; at least she seemed to understand me at first. One day I took her down to the docks and explained to her that I wanted to leave on one of the ships. She said that I was childish and that I couldn't face reality. She told me that I had to work hard for what I wanted and couldn't run away from myself. I guess she thought I was just a little strung out because she took me up to her place then and made love to me. Afterwards she said, wasn't that nice? I said, yes that was nice, but I still didn't know what to do, and she got mad. I liked her so I listened to her, but I thought that she was wrong. I begged her to understand, but she said, let's just forget it, and we never saw each other again. That's really what did it, I think. She was like the rest of them after all. I quit my job at the warehouse but I still kept going to the harbor. One day I went onboard one of the ships, and I don't remember how it happened but I heard that it was leaving, so I just stayed on board. I didn't know where it was going but I didn't care either. I hid among some boxes and stayed there for two days until I got so hungry I couldn't stand it. I started to wonder if Andrea (the girl) had been right after all. I felt like a fool sitting between two stacks of boxes, starving to death. I wanted to keep going but I was afraid. I started to cry, I think, and someone found me. I tried to explain why I was there, but I couldn't get the words out. They left me off somewhere (San Diego) and after going to the police station I was finally brought here. Guess they didn't know what else to do with me. No one would listen to me, I remember that. They said that I was sick and I said that they were sick—the more I argued the "sicker" I was. I said that if they would let me out of here I'd go back to college. Or back to work. I'd do whatever they wanted. They asked me what *I* wanted, and I guess I made a big mistake. I told them the truth. I said I didn't know or care, but I wanted out.

"Maybe I really am crazy and do belong here. If I can't face reality like they say I guess I am a schizo-phrenic. If I say I'm well they tell me I only think so because I'm sick. If I say, O.K., I'm sick, they say, yes that's why you're here.

"If I only knew who's right. But I can't help thinking I don't belong here. I may be confused, but I'm not crazy. I don't do crazy things like some of the people here. If I stay here much longer though I'm sure I will go crazy . . . ."

The young man was obviously confused and distraught. But he was almost certainly more harmed than helped by being certified "insane." (He was subsequently given extensive shock therapy.)

Often the labelled deviant is only the most visible member—or even the scapegoat—in a sick or otherwise inadequate interpersonal net. Someone who suffers mental disturbance may be "the first one to crack" in an unhappy and tension-ridden family. If a man goes mad or a youth goes bad, someone or something must have driven him there. And if a married person is unfaithful, don't we have to ask if the spouse might be partly responsible? Perhaps the labelling of deviants is such a common social practice because it lets the rest of the people off the hook by directing attention to a defined culprit.

CHAPTER FIVE

GOING

DEVIANT

At one time or another almost every human condition and social factor has been put forward as the cause of deviance. Nearly every aspect of modern life—such as urbanism, religious freedom, ease of transportation, the flowering of science—has been accused of rending the fabric of society and setting the populace adrift on a sea of immorality. Everything from a tainting of the gene pool to a basic illness of the society itself has been blamed for contemporary "waywardness"—the coddling of youth and the neglect of youth, poverty and affluence, authoritarianism and permissiveness, the growth of secular rationality and the decline of secular rationality, too much freedom and too many pressures to conform.

But all these explanations are inadequate for one or two reasons. First, the alleged cause of deviance is really only a synonym for it. For example, writers see many commonplace aspects of urban life as deviant and then impute the rise of deviance to the rise of urbanism.

Or they regard the wilfulness of youth as deviant and they blame the deviance of youth on their increasing wilfulness. The assertion that deviants are produced by socially disorganized areas is also circular since areas are defined as organized or disorganized by their deviance rates. And as we've seen, "explaining" with such terms as "psychopath" involves little more than name-calling.

The second inadequacy of explanations for deviance is logical. Some people influenced by causal factor X aren't deviant, while some people not influenced by X are deviant. A cause, or even a contributing factor, at least must have a strong relationship to deviance; where there is deviance there too is factor X. But the host of empirical studies comparing deviants and nondeviants has failed to establish any such relationships.

Deviance is a diverse phenomenon with diverse causes. Sometimes there is biological anomaly, sometimes a disrupted home, sometimes bad companions, sometimes too little legitimate opportunity, sometimes too much pressure, and so on. *Since virtually any behavior is deviant from the moral perspective of some judge, virtually everything causes deviance.* That is, since deviant behavior includes virtually all human behavior, its causes are the causes of all human behaviors. The inventory of causes that applies to particular cases must include the entire range of physical conditions, human emotions, and social forces which influence human behavior generally.

All of this suggests that we may be asking the wrong questions about the origins of deviance. Each of the factors which have been suggested in the past will be valid for some individual cases but none is very useful for explaining the general thing. Multiple-causation theories (poverty plus broken home plus bad companions plus psychopathic tendencies plus a growing godlessness) only compound this problem instead of solve it, as Albert Cohen has pointed out.

Going deviant seems to be best understood as a process involving an interplay between a person's ongoing behavior and all the social forces surrounding this behavior. It is not caused by either; rather it emerges from the interrelationships between both. For example, David Matza has shown that delinquents drift back and forth between conventionality and crime; they are neither wholeheartedly opposed to the Establishment nor wholeheartedly in favor of lawlessness. Only a tiny fraction of deviants would endorse a complete overthrow of the present society and moral order. In fact, a good deal of the deviant's internal turmoil stems from his fundamental attachment to a society which continually condemns him.

Why do some people take a deviant path, knowing something of its turmoils and the society's highly negative attitudes? Why would anyone put himself in such a miserable position? To understand this process we must look at the world through the eyes of the person surveying his environment and going deviant. *From his or her viewpoint* there must be advantages. Or little choice. Either way, the regular paths of self-realization, of survival and success, are somehow barred, at least within the person's mind.

Just about everyone has probably stood many times at the crossroads between deviance and conventionality, mentally and emotionally confused about which way to go. We could as easily be asking why people conform as why people deviate. If we open our minds and step back a little from our own moral preconceptions we can begin to see why deviating can "make more sense" for some persons under some circumstances than complying with society.

Sometimes people will experiment with deviance not because of greater advantages but because they have become alienated from the conventional society. Jackman, O'Toole, and Geis found that girls entering prostitution were isolated and alienated from the constraints of middle-class morality. And Lewis Yablonsky reports the reason a youngster joined a "gang war" though not a gang member: "My folks threw me out of the house; I wanted to get somebody and heard about the fight."

People will sometimes be deviate in an attempt to "work through" repressions, neuroses, and hangups. I think the bulk of experimental deviance takes this form, just as most people will, sometime in their lives, fulfill a dream of gorging themselves on candy or ice cream. If left to run its natural course, such a fulfilled desire will usually burn itself out quickly. But if impeded it is likely to become a fixed obsession, compulsively repeated for its partial satisfactions. And if society condemns and stigmatizes these experimentations, a youth, for example, may be unable to either work anything out or very easily stop the "experiment." If the society is permissive, these workings through will be pranks and "crimes without victims"; if the society is suppressive, they will become antagonistic and antisocial.

THE COMMITTING OF DEVIANT ACTS

A "voluntary act" requires, in simplest terms, a desire and an opportunity. Both must be present to some extent but their inter-relationship is complicated. A person won't act upon a slight desire unless the opportunity before him is especially great, and, conversely, someone who is fiercely willing is likely to act upon the slightest opportunity.

As Richard Cloward and others have pointed out, some of the opportunities before a person are legitimate and some are illegitimate from the standpoint of the effective majority in that scene. People are constrained from crossing over into the illicit zone because of their own moral training and through fear of retribution, but the constraint is never complete. The overwhelming majority of the population is ambivalent about conventionality and about deviations from official ideals. This ambivalence may be so slight that it never even appears under ordinary circumstances; some members of the group may live their entire lifetime without showing much of it. But the number of such utterly solid citizens may be much smaller than we ordinarily think.

The more extreme the circumstances, the "farther out" people will go along the line from the official ideals to the conventional divergences, into the zone of deviance. The extremity leading people to deviate may be either an exceptional opportunity (a really big chance, a really large sum of money, a really beautiful girl) or a situation of dire threat. The public and the courts usually take into consideration circumstances as well as behavior itself when judging an individual. The more extenuating the circumstances, the more diver-gent the behavior that will be tolerated. Fear or rage can suddenly make a conformer a killer, a turncoat, a thief. What would you do for a clear million dollars? To save your family's lives? To save yourself?

If a person belongs to a group whose standards conflict with those of the effective majority, he will deviate merely by "being himself" in that scene. But his ambivalence will be even sharper and more poignant because, having learned the values of the larger society, he'll be betraying somebody's expectations whatever he does. Cynicism and apathy are frequent outcomes of such moral cross-pressures.

In modern societies, where there is so much information and moral controversy among divergent groups, the conventional person will in turn learn something about some of the deviant subcultures around him. With this preparation most of the conventional populace is "seduceable" to some deviance just as the members of the deviant subcultures are varingly amenable to recruitment into conventionality. In our final pilot study we included three questions to test "seduce-ability": If given the chance, would you spend an evening in a beatnik hangout? Try a harmless dose of narcotics? Have an extra-marital affair? The most common response on all three questions was "I would think about it, but probably wouldn't do it." Only a small minority dismissed all three possibilities out of hand.

Put simply, this is the essence of the "differential association theory" of criminality introduced by Sutherland and elaborated by Cressey, Glaser, and others. Deviant behavior results from a net excess of deviant over nondeviant social influences and opportunities. Since conventional people provide deviant as well as nondeviant influences and opportunities, and since deviants provide conventional as well as deviant influences, *virtually no one will incorporate entirely conventional or entirely deviant attitudes.*

It's interesting to contemplate the fact that even the most sheltered members of our society have learned a certain amount of unconventionality from the very solid citizens who sheltered and restricted them. It suggests that virtually everyone is a potential deviant. The widespread idea that the population is composed of a hard deviant core, a fringe of enticeable "latent deviants" and a vast bulk of irreproachable citizens is therefore a myth.

But the real importance of this ambivalence is that rates of deviance are quite sensitive to situational influences. When social conditions change, the number of deviant acts will change even if attitudes remain constant because there will be a shift in the definitions of legitimate and illegitimate opportunities. Contraception and co-education thus increased illicit sexual liaisons before there was much change in sexual attitudes. If public attitudes change, deviance rates will also change even if opportunities remain the same; people will be either more motivated or less motivated to act than they were before. And if enough people change their attitudes there'll be a change in what is generally considered deviant. But behavior changes in response to changing opportunities often come before any general shift in attitudes. This is true of premarital sex and marijuana smoking in our own time. Needless to say, when someone's behavior changes before his attitudes, he can be torn by internal conflicts.

Consider these reminiscences of a university coed:

Margie was pacing about my office, restlessly looking over the books and out the windows. She turned back and looked at me almost defiantly. "I really do think all Americans are screwed up about sex, at least everybody I ever met."

"How's that?"

"Well—just about every girl I know who enjoys sex and making love has gone through a time when they worried about being nymphomanic or sick or dirty or something. And guys are all hung up too; you wouldn't believe what you run into with guys."

"What do you think the screw up is?"

"Our heads are in a place where nobody can have love, make love without being uptight. We're scared of sex and we're scared of other people. I don't know, but it isn't the way it should be."

"How do you think we got this way?"

"Oh it's our famous upbringing. It's taken me a long time to get out from underneath my upbringing and I'm not over it yet. Ever think how people try to force everybody else to have their own sex hangups? When I was growing up my folks told me that if a boy really likes and respects you he won't want to touch you. How's that for double-think? Think what it does to your mind every time they shake their finger at you." She shook her finger and made a face.

"Do you think girls come off worse than guys in upbringing?"

She looked pensively out the window. "I think so. Girls really are taught to be paranoid about the big wide world so we're sorta crippled by that. We get so defensive that we grab onto the first half-decent boy we run into. It makes us dependent persons. But boys get caught in the trap too. The double-standard messes their mind up a lot. I remember high school boys were always so clumsy and ashamed of themselves when they wanted to get intimate with a girl. That's sad."

"Do you think this generation is freer about sex than the last one?"

"Oh yes. Well . . . I don't really know how much though. Like this place is supposed to be a playground by the ocean, but I could show you a lot of lonely, screwed-up people. Our society's so hysterical about dirty that you can't just walk away from it. We talk pretty openly and I think we are more open too. But it's . . . unstable, you never know when somebody's going to turn around and call you an easy screw or a pervert. And everybody still giggles about sleeping together and Greek love, French love, you know, oral-genital sex." She giggled.

"You think students are hung up about oral-genital sex?"

"I certainly do. One way or the other. That's what happens with hangups, you usually flip out one way or the other. I know this girl who has never ever had straight sex but she always, you know, goes down with boys. She has a climax when the guy does but she doesn't let them touch her. It's really weird because she puts down girls who sleep around. And the guys she goes out with talk about her and put her down."

"I see what you mean about the hangup."

"I was hung up too for a long time. I know I still am a little. I don't think *any* of us are as emancipated as we'd like to think. I remember wondering when I was in high school whether couples would get up and go to the icebox for a midnight snack after they'd eaten each other. I remember dreaming that a guy forced me to do that for him, it was really scary and exciting at the same time. When I finally did it with a boy I liked it was really funny sitting across the table from my folks in the morning, listening to them chit-chat. Say, are you going to put this all in your book?"

"I don't know yet."

"You know I haven't really done that much. My boyfriend and I are really sorta giving therapy to each other more than going with each other." She shuddered. "It scares me to think sometimes what I'd be like now if I hadn't met some different people. Now I've got the chance to be alive."

Two major processes create deviant acts and, eventually, a full-fledged deviant. First, a number of factors combining to encourage people to experiment with deviance can be called "role-recruitment." Second is the process that forces some people into deviant acts, especially forces on those who already have experimented with deviance to adopt and maintain a deviant role. That process can be called "role-imprisonment."

Most people try liquor before they are of legal age, but only a few become alcoholics. Most of us have, at one time or another, become quite disturbed emotionally, yet only a few of us become mentally ill. And most people have experimented with illicit sexual behaviors, yet only a fraction actually become sexual deviants. Committing a deviant act at some time is not a sufficient condition for really going deviant but it is a necessary step and more; it shifts around the likelihood of various possibilities in the person's future. However, it shouldn't be thought of as the starting point in becoming deviant because both recruitment processes and imprisonment processes have already been actively influencing the person long before he commits his first deviant act.

DEVIANCE RECRUITMENT PROCESSES

As Howard Becker and others have demonstrated, one of the most effective social obstacles on the deviant path is the negative stereotype of deviance absorbed from childhood even by deviants and which even they seldom question. From a thousand admonitions, stories, and offhand remarks we absorb a composite image of the deviant as a less-than-human creature skulking beyond the light of society, driven on by uncontrollable perversities, repulsive, self-loathing, and ultimately tragic. When the thought of violating the local moral standards arises, this image also arises, to keep the majority in line. After all, who wants to become a less-than-human creature? But even a person willing to risk this has also been taught that all those who deviate are inevitably discovered, publicly condemned, and punished. If a deviant manages to escape detection by the ordinary forces of society, he still dreads eventual retribution at the hands of some higher court—Fate or the gods or Poetic Justice.

People who firmly believe such stereotypes are very unlikely to commit deviant acts, unless they are so distraught or alienated that they "volunteer" to accept this image as a kind of suicidal gesture. Edwin Lemert has shown, for example, that check forgers often behave in a manner that can only increase the likelihood of their being caught and punished. I've seen the same recklessness among some illegal drug dealers and adulterers. A dean of women at a Midwestern university told me that many girls who came to her attention seemed bent upon getting themselves pregnant and publicly disgraced.

But such self-punishing cases seem to be the minority in most types of deviance. The vast bulk of deviants strayed beyond the boundaries of acceptable divergence only after their belief in the negative stereotypes and inevitable retribution had disintegrated—at least to some extent. As the grip of these negative conceptions weakens the very same opportunities to deviate become more attractive than before because the risk will appear less.

The process of weakening negative conceptions can be seen in the case of a youth who arrived from a small town to attend one of the West Coast universities and who eventually took up the regular use of marijuana.

> When he came onto the campus in the mid-60's he simply accepted the prevailing image of pot as a danger-ous drug that stripped people of their senses and ushered them into the grey Hell of hopeless drug addiction. He heard from other freshmen and some older students in the church youth group he joined that a lot of the "fringies" were using drugs and that they were all "going to get busted" and sent to prison. He'd read William Burrough's *Naked Lunch* the summer before and had no inclination to try anything more than the beer that was everpresent in his circle of acquaintances. The fringies sat in their own corner of the student union, shunned by most of the other students because they were so strange and because of fears about getting a bad reputation by even being seen with them. And so his first year went by with fairly good grades, pleasant dating, and bull sessions about the Meaning of It All.
>
> He had been assistant editor of his high school news-paper and in the fall of his second year he started working as a photographer on the student daily. This brought him into contact with many of the inner circles

of the student body, and he discovered there was a far wider range of opinions about drugs, sex, politics, and so on than had existed in his church youth group or among his beer buddies. He noticed too that the fringie corner had swelled considerably and that straight-looking girls were beginning to walk openly across campus with some of the long-haired males. The group began to arouse his curiousity and one afternoon he summoned up the courage to go over and sit at one of "their" tables where a half dozen of "them" were lounging around. The talk seemed to stop abruptly as he sat down and he had, for one of the first times in his life, the uncomfortable feeling of being the outsider. After pretending to read his textbook for a few minutes he got up and fled.

Almost without realizing it he fell into a relationship with one of the girls working on the paper. She was a senior who turned on with marijuana occasionally and who had many acquaintances using it regularly. This was a magic period in his life—the girl led him into sexual intimacies that were at first crude and confusing ("like wrestling with my roommate") but which became more and more satisfying and beautiful to him. The pair was welcome at many of the apartments around the campus and he was excited with the first flush of being in on the scenes where everything seemed to be happening.

The first time he tried marijuana nothing seemed to happen except that his skin "felt furry" for a little while. He couldn't shake off the feeling that he was on a path of degradation and he felt very paranoid about people knowing that he'd tried the drug. Toward spring the girl left him for a political science grad student and he discovered that their friends had been more hers than his. He felt alone and lost and his grades suffered. He spoke bitterly about the student fringe to his old beer drinking companions, but he found that they now bored him with their loud pretenses of masculinity and their still adolescent sexual attitudes and political views. So he withdrew into himself and read a string of "life's a horror show" novels that agreed with his mood.

He spent a silent summer at home with his folks. But he discovered something which surprised him. One night on television a police officer and a panel moderator denounced the menacing epidemic of marijuana use and, remembering his former acquaintances, he became indignant at the false picture they were painting. The people living in those off-campus apartments weren't anything like what the panelists were so learnedly describing. In talking with his parents and the relatives who came to visit he found himself defending those he'd previously denounced, and he had his first real inkling that something larger than his own personal quest was going on.

He went back to classes and to the paper that fall with clearer feelings about where his own allegiances were. He fell in with the liberal civil rights crowd which was something of a liaison between the still growing fringe and the rest of the student body. He was surprised to find out how many of his new straight-looking friends and acquaintances had tried pot or were using it off and on. The second time he tried it, nothing seemed to be happening for awhile but he soon found himself stretched out on the apartment floor listening to records. He began to feel "inside" the music in a way he never had before. The Stones, Dylan, The Beatles, and Donavon were all expressing meanings and nuances he'd never heard before, although he'd heard these records many times. From then on he nearly always accepted offers of pot. But still fearful of being caught, he didn't keep any marijuana on hand himself.

He became acquainted with some of the fringe group but still felt uncomfortable with them and still couldn't understand or go along with much of what they said and did. Still they were fascinating to know and he agreed with many of their complaints about society in the same way he had agreed with the nihilistic novels of his previous year. He dated casually and "messed around" but couldn't find a girl he really connected with. One night, during the winter quarter, he got especially stoned after successfully weathering a tough round of midterm tests. A dark-haired girl whom he'd met a couple times before was there among the dozen or so other students. "We were listening to the music together and then we just sort of got up and went into the other room. It was so simple, no games or bribes or anything that went along with the old dating scene. Her hair was all over my face like a tent; we just melted together into a warm puddle. When I woke up later she said 'hi' and it was the most honest hello anybody ever said to me in my life."

A few of his acquaintances were using heroin off and on, but the haunted look in their eyes stopped him from even wanting to try it. Somebody (it was rumored to be organized crime) had made a lot of heroin available for virtually nothing, but only the few who just didn't seem to care anymore about anything wanted to experiment with it. "Society had lied to us about pot and I wondered if they were lying about heroin too. But I never ran into a happy smack-head. We pretty much broke off from anybody who was shooting up."

He started getting some campus recognition for his articles but he now associated mainly with other marijuana users. The main bond among them was the fact that they were sharing the same experiences and facing the same problems of procuring the drug and evading the authorities. "In those days other potheads were your automatic brothers." His doubts about the drug had entirely vanished but he still felt wary because of its illegality.

In his senior year the former fringe had grown to a sizeable minority and were now at the center of the student body. Straight students were now called "soshes" and their position of supremacy in campus affairs had been usurped. He has now found a comfortable and satisfying way of life, but he has misgivings about entering the "square" adult world upon graduation. He doubts he'll ever stop using marijuana, whether it's legalized or not. And he can't imagine marrying a girl who doesn't turn on. "It would be like marrying a deaf-mute."

When someone successfully completes a deviant act—carried away by an exceedingly attractive opportunity or especially strong desires or intense group pressures—the hold of the negative stereotypes weakens. A person learns by direct experience that deviance is not a strange and twisted world beyond the pale of ordinary men, and that those who commit deviant acts are fundamentally just people. Kinsey found that among women who had had premarital sex, guilt and regret diminished as experience increased. Each subsequent deviant act further weakens the stereotypes in the person's mind, although it takes a long time for them to dissipate entirely. Often they never do.

Dread of discovery and retribution also recede as the fledgling deviant sees that he and his companions remain undetected and unpunished. He becomes far more ready to act upon illicit opportunities, although some shadow of former dread is likely to return now and again as acquaintances "get busted." This growing sense of security is sometimes false, but it is more accurate than the stereotypes. After all, most deviants don't get caught.

However, the "successful" commission of deviant acts sometimes has other results. The experience can arouse such anxieties and negative self-feelings that they reinforce rather than weaken the negative stereotypes; the person feels afterwards that he narrowly escaped an unholy fate. Several respondents said they were so shamed, disgusted, or terrified by experimentations with deviance that they have since rejected all such possibilities out of hand. But these were a small minority. If the first fumbling attempt is unsuccessful—if the drug experience is terrifying, if the illicit sexual encounter is a clumsy fiasco, if running away from home leads only to loneliness and misery—it is likely to turn the person against future illicit opportunities. A number of informants reported essentially this course of flirtation with drugs, homosexuality, interracial love affairs, and extremist politics. One doesn't become a marijuana smoker, a philanderer, a hippie merely by wishing to do so. We are sometimes tempted from a distance by the idea of illicit actions, but the raw realities of even the preliminaries to the act frequently prove so complicated and upsetting that we draw back and return to conventionality.

The successful completion of one or a few deviant acts usually greatly reduces the person's doubts and fears. Furthermore, the illicit opportunities for subsequent safer deviance will usually increase. The person knows where to go and what to do. If other people are involved they'll be likely to supply further opportunities on the basis of past success. Conventional and deviant behaviors are alike in that success leads to competence and reputation and makes further success easier.

Other people are crucial in the processes of recruitment into deviance. These others provide illicit opportunities for several reasons: their own pleasure-seeking, as in sexual partnerships; simple profit, as in drug sale or prostitution; or the power of numbers, as in fringe groups and revolutionary movements.

The classic profit motive may lead others to offer illicit opportunities, especially when illegal organizations have sprung up to service deviance. Such organizations are interested in recruiting new customers exactly as are department stores or banks. In each case the profit motive leads the "businessman" to encourage and seduce people to sample his wares and, hopefully, to become steady customers. Ironically organized crime embodies many of the characteristics admired in ordinary business entrepeneurs.

Most commonly, however, individuals and groups simply want more people to share their deviant activities or fringe views. Almost all groups, deviant or nondeviant, are on the lookout for promising newcomers who meet their standards. The Democratic Party and the Hells Angels, the PTA and the Black Panthers all spend missionary efforts to increase their numbers. But the recruiting by deviants isn't just a seduction of the innocent by the forces of darkness. The new recruit is not shanghaied, but seeks whatever the group offers. Whether such conversions are bad or good depends on where you stand—one group's turncoat is the other group's loyal new member.

The simplest and truest reason the person accepts recruitment into deviance is that he finds it rewarding. In the spinning of elaborate psychological and sociological theories this fact is too often overlooked. Several years ago a lesbian interrupted my interview with her and said, "We've kept talking about emotional turmoil and male avoidance. But the truth is I go to bed with her because it's fun."

A certain fraction of the people who experiment with deviant activities find behaviors that are more satisfying and meaningful and so they want to adopt these patterns. After all, the rules are fetters as well as guidelines and each of us carries some burden of discontent and dissatisfaction. We are all only more or less satisfied with the way things are for us. And so it isn't surprising that some who experiment with deviance find a more fulfilling niche "out there."

DEVIANT ROLE-IMPRISONMENT PROCESSES

Even before their first deviant act, certain people are, willy-nilly, turning toward deviance. Certain role-imprisonment processes, in some cases merely facets of the role-recruitment processes discussed above, are responsible. For instance, the reward of easing anxiety with alcohol can build first a habit and then a necessity for using alcohol at the first appearance of stress. But there are some unique additional aspects to being imprisoned in deviance.

Belonging to a group with standards and ideas that run contrary to mainstream society can spell both recruitment and imprisonment, especially if the person has been raised in that setting. Deviance becomes part of his growing up. The imprisoning features of this situation so common in the ghetto are that the person will find it extremely difficult to break out and make his way in the larger society. His past upbringing and "deviant" record make him an ill-suited newcomer by the standards of the society he hopes to join.

Those who belong to the more disprivileged classes in a society are imprisoned in a double discrimination. First, there is discrimination in the enforcement of the rules. Many researchers have demonstrated such bias in police departments, courts, schools, mental hospitals, and so on. Beyond this, the rules themselves discriminate because they reflect the moral standards and ideology of the more privileged groups and classes. As a black militant once told me, "Whitey makes the laws we gotta live by." The point is that the disprivileged may be imprisoned in deviance unwillingly or even unaware merely because they do not (by definition) have an equal voice in shaping the rules and standards under which all must live *and all are evaluated*. The person can, of course, try to live by the standards of the majority but this will entail, at the very least, a period of marginality during which his relationships with his disprivileged group are strained while his footing in the larger society is still uncertain. The assertion, often made by members of more privileged groups, that anyone who really wants to can climb out of poverty and disadvantage is naive and supercilious.

There are a number of other imprisonment processes which usually come into play only among those who have already committed deviant acts. These are the subtle interpersonal processes by which we tend to become what other people think we are. Given the name, we are likely to adopt the game, not only because other games will consequently be less available to us but because we all tend to weave the judgments of others into our own self-image. For example, if a high school girl develops a reputation of being "loose" as a result of being carried away one evening she may find it very hard not to be loose as she receives fewer and fewer "honorable" offers. When the other boys and girls in her high school behave as if she were loose, the probability increases that she will play out the part assigned her.

Imprisonment processes usually operate, then, after people have been recruited into deviance. Deviance, like marriage, is almost always far easier to get into than get out of. Deviance-imprisonment processes work mainly through drastically altering the field of legitimate and illicit opportunities open to the person. Seldom are particular future paths entirely ruled out or entirely predestined; the "imprisonment" is almost never total. But the probabilities shift through the accumulation of a history or "record."

THE ACCUMULATION OF TRACES

Role-imprisonment curtails a person's freedom to choose between deviance and nondeviance. Entirely independent of motives and habits, deviant acts leave an inevitable accumulation of traces.

Most human behavior leaves traces of some kind—signatures, overheard talk and accidental observance, smells, smears, conspicuous absences, remembered purchases, long-distance logs, and so on and on. Individual traces may be completely innocuous or easily explained away. But certain people are in a position to accumulate such traces until they are led to the correct conclusion about what the person is up to. Not only the police, but janitors, waitresses, bartenders, neighbors, are examples of such people. Also, whenever people come together socially they almost inevitably talk about others. At such meetings single traces known to different people may be put together.

A good many of the deviant respondents in our studies said they had once been very naive about the invisibility of their activities. Most of them had had to learn about traces the hard way and they gave an interesting list of examples that had at one time or another given them away: places their cars were parked, buildings they were seen entering and leaving at certain times, facial expressions during various topics of casual conversation, the exchange of glances with others, mussed hair, matchbooks they were carrying, a shift from their usual daily habits, inadvertently revealed knowledge of places or events outside their usual haunts, unusually extensive knowledge about certain people, lost buttons and bobbypins, undue weariness or defensiveness, coffee-break companions, contents of their garbage cans, neighborhood shopping center purchases, overheard phone conversations, and so on.

Single traces are usually ambiguous but as they accumulate they become more and more reliable indicators. Because this is especially true when the deviant stays around the same small town or the same urban neighborhood for a time, many deviants move regularly. Otherwise the accumulation of some kind of a local "record" is almost inevitable.

Most people could be embarrassed by a thorough but routine investigation. Contrary to popular conceptions in spy and detective fiction, the investigation of a person's private life is not a matter of bravado or brilliant deducing. In almost all real-life instances it involves the methodical and exhaustive application of clerical and case-work skills—the legwork of examining a lot of records and asking a lot of humdrum questions. The standard operating principle of governmental security agencies is that you can find out as much as you want about somebody if you're willing to spend the money. Such agencies have found that even superficial interview responses become quite revealing when put together.

Historically, most people have been under the constant surveillance of their families and fellow tribesmen. The whole community kept their "records" as public knowledge. More recently people could escape such fetters with relative ease by moving on and starting afresh. But in our own time this increased freedom from one's past is again threatened by the ever-increasing practice of routinely recording and compiling more and more of the facts of peoples' lives. School records, medical histories, military service records, work records, income statements, credit records, residence histories, and so on are being gathered systematically for virtually everyone in most modern societies. And these records are becoming increasingly available to any "authorized" person or agency, including credit bureaus, prospective employers and landlords, and investigating committees. The spread of computer files is greatly accelerating this practice. This trend raises new long-term concealment problems for the deviant and makes post-prison or post-mental hospital return to conventionality more difficult.

But traces of deviance do tend to fade with time. Memories weaken and old records are destroyed. People are not held so accountable for their distant pasts. There is a statute of limitations preventing prosecuting of most crimes after the lapse of a specified period of time. And the practice of holding people accountable only for behavior of the recent past seems to be growing as a result of the increasingly accepted view that people do change. "Once a junkie, always a junkie," "once a schitz, always a schitz," "once a thief, always a thief" are still widespread beliefs but they are not nearly as universal as they once were. No longer is it so taken for granted that one deviant act is the symptom of a basic character taint that must run its dark course. But this shift in attitudes is only in its beginnings and many a deviant is still tyrannized by his past.

Inferences drawn from traces are, of course, not necessarily accurate. People are sometimes falsely stigmatized on the basis of false inferences from shadowy evidence, while others who do engage in deviance have the skill or good fortune to not leave enough traces to give themselves away. Many people have succeeded in concealing a long history of sporadic deviant activities from the public. Over the past few years the deviants I interviewed included many who had kept their deviance secret for a long time. However, in each case I think that a determined investigation would have revealed their secrets.

If traces are so durable and so damning, how can it be that most deviants are not caught? Part of the answer is a matter of sheer numbers. To apprehend, try, and treat all the marijuana users or homosexuals or delinquents in our society, for example, would require staggering energies and resources. Expenditures exceeding our entire defense budget would probably be necessary for an indefinite period. Most people would also probably feel that we have better things to do and so the necessary massive popular support would be lacking.

Also there is the matter of being cool. Traces can be minimized by ordinary discretion. Again and again, deviant respondents told of acquaintances who were "busted" or otherwise came to grief because they didn't lower the blinds, because they ran a red light or drove a car with faulty equipment, because they wrote checks instead of paying cash for illicit services, because they turned on or went to bed with uncool and unknown people, because they talked too much, because they didn't clean up, or because they failed to stash illegal articles.

There is also the fact that suspicion is not proof. Often it is not even sufficient grounds for issuing a search warrant, suspending a student, or firing an employee. In the majority of cases the inferences made from traces are, at best, only circumstantial evidence. Veteran deviants often survive a general consensus of opinion against them by sticking to a "straight" story, since the burden of proof usually rests with the accusers. Police, administrators, and other informed parties often construct a very detailed and accurate picture of what's going on within their purview, but the evidence is not strong enough to act upon or is obtained illegally.

Since the majority of deviants engage in illicit activities only sporadically, their traces are fairly widely separated over space and time, making them hard to build into condemning evidence. Whether this is a deliberate ploy or merely necessitated by nondeviant commitments and involvements, it serves to minimize risks.

Large numbers of people can thus occasionally deviate with relative impunity. But if discovered, a temporary deviant may be put in such a position that he can hardly refrain from deviance in the future. Identified as a deviant, nondeviant opportunities frequently become less available to him. If officially punished or treated, he often finds that the only place he can now go is back into the milieu which nurtured his deviance in the first place.

Apprehension or informal stigmatization may begin a cycle of further entrenchment, producing a full-fledged deviant. Someone who has been recruited and/or imprisoned in deviance will thus often have his ordinary conventional roles altered to accommodate a more thoroughgoing deviant life-style. In time the opportunities and the motivation to break out of his deviant life-style recede. If he is at all successful in pursuing this new way of life he may come to find it more and more rewarding and less and less painful or difficult to manage. Conventional influences upon him fade. Finally the fledgling experimenter becomes a full-fledged deviant.

THE RISKS OF GOING DEVIANT

What are the risks involved in going deviant? What truth is there in the popular stereotype of the deviant life as nasty, brutish, and short?

This is a relative matter since all human enterprises, conventional or deviant, entail risks and costs. Our question is really a statistical one: Do deviant careers entail more (or less) risks than conventional careers?

We must also ask whether the risks and costs of some particular deviance are greater (or less) than the alternatives. For example, are the hazards of smoking marijuana greater than the hazards of drinking alcohol? To take another example, the children of wealthy families are often sent to exclusive schools where they are carefully chaperoned and kept from intermingling with the opposite sex. But studies have revealed that the advantages of such schools are balanced by the risk of homosexuality which is rampant in such schools.

There are no comparative statistics so our questions can't be fully answered. But a few points can be made. Deviance is a riskier business than conventionality—but nowhere near as risky as the popular stereotype. If deviance really were as risky as is conventionally portrayed, there would be few if any deviants. Obviously this is not the case.

Most of those who commit deviant acts are never caught or arrested. And the majority of those who are arrested might have "failed" in conventional endeavors as well. Many people do get trapped in some form of deviance, but they are only a small minority of deviants. And deviants have no monopoly on living trapped lives or being hooked on questionable and even dangerous things.

Some deviants come to grief. But many upright people who do what they are supposed to and never stray from the path of conventionality also come to grief. I don't think there's any doubt that the deviant's life tends to be somewhat harsher and more uncertain. But life is something of a gamble for all of us so that any differences between deviance and conformity are only a matter of degree or "odds."

How about the risk of personal harm? For instance, does drinking involve greater expense, health hazard, likelihood of accidents, or even risk of arrest than smoking marijuana? Are the hazards of dropping out greater than the hazards of the ratrace? Are the possible side-effects of using LSD (emotional disturbance, possibly deteriorative diseases) greater than the risks of nonuse (mental disturbance, possibly the deteriorative diseases)? Does widespread sexual abandonment cause more personal or social harm than widespread sexual frustration? We don't know yet, but we should pose these kinds of comparative and balanced questions to find out.

The popular stereotype about the grave hazards and untimely fall of the deviant probably arises from a universal bias. Every society seems to grossly exaggerrate the terrors and risks of what is disapproved of and to minimize the risks of approved and encouraged behavior. But in reality deviance isn't all that deadly and conventionality isn't all that safe. Timothy Leary is probably right when he says graduate school causes as much insanity and suicide as psychedelic drugs. Our industries are probably spreading as much poisonous waste and causing more injuries and deaths with unsafe products than the Mafia. But still the effective majority feels that the merits of graduate school and industry make these risks worthwhile.

CHAPTER SIX

INTERPERSONAL

PROBLEMS

The deviant does not live in a social vacuum. Both his behavior and his internal psychological processes are colored by the fact that his activities are taboo. At least some of the people who are influential in his particular scene, if they knew, would vilify and perhaps punish him.

All human beings must face the existential problems of somehow making their way in the world—of procuring what they need and want, of getting along with the people around them, and of maintaining themselves psychologically. But these human problems are compounded and they take on somewhat special forms for the deviant because of the widespread negative attitudes toward what he or she is doing. Even when a person's deviance is not publicly known, there are legal and social controls which must be circumvented, and the threat of discovery and retribution are very real threats. If, in turnabout fashion, we attempt to look at conventional society through the eyes of the deviant we can really begin to understand the impact of the public attitudes discussed earlier. And we can see how much of the alienation, self-condemnation, paranoia, and desperation found among deviants is the self-fulfilling result of these public images.

How do people manage their deviant activities, along with their ordinary conventional involvements, in the face of a disapproving society?

One of the sharpest differences between deviance and conventionality is in procuring the necessary goods and services. It seems that society's second line of defense against deviance (after the negative stereotypes) is the attempt, along many different levels, to cut off illicit supplies and services and thus cut off deviant opportunities. This is seen as a more efficient way of curbing deviance than trying to round up and treat the legions of individual culprits. On the other hand, society fosters conventional activities, albeit for a price.

Think, for instance, of the differences between having a baby and having an illegal abortion. One occurs with the blessings and cooperation of family and friends, the medical profession and society. The other occurs in haste and secrecy, with little support and dubious competence.

Or compare the situation of a white married couple with that of a black man living with a white girl. The married couple enjoys the approval and aid of a whole range of social institutions, and the whole society wishes them well. The unmarried pair can look forward to constant informal, and perhaps official harrassment. They must be evasive and they have few resources to lean upon outside themselves.

Or compare the person who likes tobacco with the person who likes marijuana. The former can rely upon hundreds of thousands of cigarette counters and vending machines all over the country. Wherever he goes he is assured of a supply. He can light up almost anytime, anywhere. He doesn't have to hope the sales clerk is cool as he is choosing from among twenty or thirty brands. There's no problem if he inadvertently drops a cigarette or leaves a butt behind in the ashtray. And his worst persecution is the nagging that can befall him by family, friend, and federal agencies about the hazards to his health.

Compare the situations of the soldier and the conscientious objector, the married schoolteacher and the lesbian schoolteacher, the Name Brands shopper and the organic health food shopper, the fashionable dresser and the nudist, someone who believes in saints and angels and someone who believes in spiritualism and telepathy.

Not that legitimate activities are supported and facilitated in all ways or that illicit courses are singlemindedly blocked by society. In some situations deviance is easier in spite of the difficulties. Homosexuality aboard ship or in a cloistered boys' school is more feasible than heterosexuality. An extramarital affair is easier than divorce and remarriage. And dealing drugs is perhaps easier than getting a regular job if you're a school dropout with a checkered work history and no diploma passport. Many of the deviant respondents reported that it was easier for them to go outside of conventionality than to remain within it. But none of them said that deviance was an easy path in the long run. Procuring goods and services is too uncertain and hazardous.

Perhaps the most fundamental and recurrent interpersonal problem of the deviant is that he or she faces the everpresent danger of retribution from the people and the official agencies in the surrounding environment. Arrest and committment of some kind are only the most extreme forms of this danger; they are the most spectacular but they really touch only a small fraction of deviants directly. Far more frequent and significant are the thousand and one daily discriminations and condemnations and hassles.

Conventional people are hardly aware of the extent to which they continuously voice and act out their moral standards. But in the act of doing so they challenge, condemn, and ostracize those who are different. The habitual deviant faces some risk of job loss, of family crises, of "referral to counselling," and even of informal physical violence. These are real threats and not infrequent actualities. But these things are only the background to the daily realities of the disapproving frown and the quizzical look, the television comedian's joke, the shushed conversations which engender the sense that you are a stranger in a strange land.

A black respondent with a white girlfriend in a small midwestern city described his double isolation:

> "When this white chick and I first started making it I felt like I'd been plunked down in the middle of Russia, like I was a spy. We got together in the first place because we were working the same restaurant but after we were sleeping together I hated to show up for work

even, and I finally quit. I had this feeling that everybody was looking. And there was no place for us to go. My people started saying 'What's the matter, why you so sulky?' We were just sitting having coffee one day and a couple of football guys come over and ask her 'Is he bothering you?' One of her roommates called up the school and turned her in to her parents and the dean. Then they all wanted her to go see a psychiatrist. We just quit going out anywhere together. We even had to split up to buy a pack of cigarettes. A patrol car stopped us one night and a cop told me I'd better hurry up and suck her out cause he was putting a curfew on us. She crying and crying and me getting mean, things you just never known about. I know who that cop is. Maybe I'll kill him someday."

Within the context of such a more or less hostile social environment the deviant must do his or her procuring and coping. Basically, this comes down to competently handling interaction situations. I am not suggesting that deviants are Machiavellian manipulators of other people. Nor am I suggesting that the deviant must incessantly cower before everpresent, immediate dangers. The deviant has his times of peace and tranquility like everyone else. The danger is not ever-present. But it is always a potential that may flare into reality at the next turn of a situation.

Of course we all learn to tread carefully in the arena of social life. We all present ourselves at least a bit differently in different situations. And we all face the job of somehow balancing the often conflicting expectations of the various other people in our lives. Rivalries and incompatibilities between the demands of dates versus parents, of colleagues versus spouses, of employers versus cronies are sometimes whimsical sometimes serious examples of this.

If a person has any reason to expect that someone important to him will condemn his ideas or activities, he must adjust for this in any interactions with that other person. This may be done to keep the benefits of a present relationship or simply to forestall antagonism. He worries even if the ideas or activities are "deviant" only to the friend or relation, not to the public in general. Thus duplicity enters into human interactions—most of us find ourselves monitoring our private feelings and intentions and tailoring them for public expression. A superficial relationship, such as customer-salesman, requires only a certain conventionality during the transaction. In more intimate relationships, however, when we know each other as individuals, we unwittingly serve as mutual watchdogs and censors. Even children and slaves have ways of reprimanding their parents and masters and so must be taken into account.

So we all must take the approvals and disapprovals of others into account. But, again, this human situation is compounded for the deviant. He must hide his deviations more carefully and systematically than the conventional person. He must maintain the good graces of those significant and influential in his situation. In addition he must placate a much larger group, those not important in his daily life but who are capable of persecuting him if they find out his "sin." Such people are everywhere—bartenders, waiters, night-clerks, landlords, bus drivers, policemen, neighbors, store managers, and passers-by. As one respondent reminisced about using marijuana in a southwestern city,

> **"I got so I just wasn't real to anybody outside of the people I was turning on with. Cooling it even with the grocery clerks is a weird way of living. I finally shaved my face and cut my hair so I could pass for straight."**

The deviant person's expectations of how others would react toward a remark or action is, of course, not necessarily accurate. Most of the respondents reported that they had made serious mistakes in gauging the reactions of others. Most were pleasantly surprised at the mild tolerance of some who had found them out. But they dwelt upon the troubles caused by underestimating the negative reactions of others.

There is a widespread popular belief among both straights and deviants that deviants are especially perceptive in seeing into and understanding people; over a third (36%) of the deviant sample spontaneously expressed this opinion at some time during the interviews. This notion of special perceptiveness makes sense since the deviant is "rewarded" for accurate appraisals and "punished" for erroneous ones. However, this widespread belief has not been empirically verified. And, in fact, I think there are grounds for asserting that deviants tend to be oversensitive, even paranoid, in their judgments of other people. The results of our interviews suggest that this diffuse paranoia and general suspiciousness arises as a reasonable defense mechanism for coping with the uncertainties of public disapproval. The classic picture of the paranoid is someone terrorized by the fear that unseen agents are plotting against him. In the case of the deviant, a moment's reflection will show that this fear is well grounded.

THE CLASSIFICATION OF OTHERS

One of the main features of modern society is the high proportion of strangers we all encounter. The conventional person can usually wend his way through these unknown people with a minimum of concern. But the deviant, if he is to survive and be socially effective, must classify all the people in his environment according to their potential threat to him. Our deviant respondents employed four rather clear-cut categories in classifying the people they encountered.

(1) Those with whom you can openly be yourself. With these people you can expect positive interactions or at least support and tolerance. They more or less accept you as you are. This group includes many, but not all, fellow deviants and some deviant in ways different from yours. For example, a homosexual, after thinking over his close friends, said that almost all of them were outside society in some way. Included were marginal and middleman people who were unconventional in their attitudes but not their behavior. The remainder were conventional people whom the deviants had learned to trust through direct experience: some teachers and clergymen, particular relatives, square but tolerant friends, and even policemen. These people often formed the links between the deviant and the rest of society. It was interesting that some of the deviant's partners were not in this first class. It was also interesting that even with this group, the trust and acceptance wasn't complete and didn't necessarily include all facets of the deviant's life.

(2) Those with whom you have friendly relations but your deviance is concealed. A handful of respondents claimed they no longer had any nondeviant associations but most said there were many people whom they were attached to and involved with, but who must be kept from knowing the "full story." Included were most relatives, many good acquaintances, teachers, employers and co-workers—in general those with whom the deviant frequently interacted in nondeviant ways. This category particularly concerned most

respondents because they were "significant others" whom the deviants didn't wish to lose or hurt. Sensing their own vulnerability to eventual discovery, many respondents said they found themselves trying either to educate these others to be more tolerant or to attenuate the relationships and replace them with people from category one.

As a side point, I have found that the majority of college students place most adults, including their parents and teachers, in category two. In a 1968 Social Change course of two hundred students, approximately eighty percent felt they needed to conceal a great deal of what they really thought and did from their folks and most other adults. About fifty-five percent said they felt isolated from adult society as a result.

(3) Those who are irrelevant or indifferent. Except for a minimal discretion, this group is largely ignored. Other people on the bus, passing pedestrians, other customers in a store are examples.

(4) Those who are a threat or potential threat. Included is most everyone in the scene who is influential and of uncertain sympathies, officials and semi-officials, anyone known or suspected to be condemning and intolerant, anyone linked with the Establishment who hasn't clearly demonstrated his acceptance and trustworthiness.

The concern these respondents had about making these classifications and the interpersonal stress they felt varied considerably. The following factors seemed to lie behind this variation.

The deviants varied greatly in the number of their deviant relationships. For those who carried out their deviance with only a minimum of contact with others, the problem of maintaining secrecy was minimal; they only needed to carefully separate their deviant and conventional activities. A political radical who wrote manuals for a large research development corporation said:

> "My output at work is almost straight Americana, it could go into the *Reader's Digest.* I kid the people at the office about reading the newspapers like they were the gospel straight from Jesus, but otherwise I just keep quiet. It pays my bills and when the whistle blows I go back to my own people."

A veteran marijuana smoker reported that he had few difficulties; it was easy to maintain a normal facade since he only used the drug when alone or with a few long-standing friends. But:

"Every so often something comes up to scare me a
little. Once my dealer got busted and I was afraid for
awhile that he'd tell who all he was selling to to get off.
And a few years ago when I started to work I got upset
about having to have a medical exam. I didn't know
much then and I remember I was afraid there'd be some
way they'd be able to tell, blood or eyes or something.
I'd heard they were supposed to report any irregularities.
I remember that I had this same vague feeling of dread
when I had to see a doctor as a kid. I was afraid they
could tell I'd been playing with my pud."

The more the content of a generally unacceptable activity requires
interaction with partners, the more complicated its maintenance
becomes. Some roles, like those of the radical or the drug users, may
not actually require interaction, but kindred spirits are desirable to
alleviate feelings of isolation and alienation, as the remarks of an
avant garde bohemian artist illustrate:

"It took a series of pitched battles, inside and out, for
me to to break out of my roots and be free. Then for a
long time I thought I didn't need people. I lived in a
monastery of my own making. But it didn't work out. I
found I need one or two friends and I also need people
to provoke me and for comic relief. So like Somerset
Maugham I stop at many tables. I'm usually disappointed
and I guess they are too. But I have to keep coming back
to people."

The respondents varied greatly in the number of their deviant
relationships. One political radical was so taciturn he rarely discussed
politics with anyone; another constantly proselytized and claimed it
had cost him two jobs and several girlfriends. One heroin user said he
spent most of his time alone; another said he was never alone. One
homosexual had lived with the same partner for over two years, had
scrupulously avoided all contact with other homosexuals, and "never
looked at another man." Another constantly sought many "rough
trade" partners, preferably new and previously heterosexual. He fre-
quented bars, hotels, and bus stations and had been arrested for
propositioning a plainclothesman.

The amount of interaction and the number of others involved in
deviant activities is therefore not simply a function of the type of
deviance. As most deviants realized, they could appreciably reduce

their contacts and more safely satisfy the bare essentials of their deviance. But they were motivated to take greater than necessary risks for the sake of greater rewards. All of them, either deliberately or unconsciously, seemed to make their decisions on the basis of an odds sheet of risks versus rewards.

Deviant activities also vary in the severity of the negative reactions they are likely to evoke upon discovery. This is partly determined by the person's position in the society: urban areas in the U.S., especially on the two coasts, are usually more tolerant than rural communities; adults are under fewer restrictions than youths; some occupations, like advertising, have more freedom than others, like high school teaching; the wealthy can afford better illicit services and protection than the poor. The knowledgeable and able deviant will thus seek situations that are tolerant and supportive of his unacceptable activities. Such moves will usually permit him to be more relaxed in his nondeviant activities as well, since the fear of discovery will haunt him less. A number of respondents said such changes, sometimes only a move to a different neighborhood or a new job-setting within the same company, had greatly relieved the strains between their deviant and nondeviant roles and had thus made their lives easier. They often advised other deviants to do the same.

However, other factors such as personal ties, career investments, or the sheer comfort of well-established routines often combine to keep the deviant in his familiar prison. A lesbian respondent said:

> "I know that some people are beginning to wonder about Carol and I. When you love someone you can't help showing it sometimes and we've begun to worry about some of the things that could happen to us. My analyst told me, why don't we go out to California and live happily ever after. (Laughs cynically.) But my job and my friends are here."

The more strongly a deviant activity is condemned, the more important is the deviant's need to accurately classify others. The mystic, the bohemian, the eccentric intellectual may experience only indifference from others or maybe a mild rejection that gives them a feeling of social isolation. The hippie and the political offbeat encounter stronger opposition and ridicule. The Negro involved with white girls, the drug user, the homosexual run greater risks of job loss, physical violence, and incarceration.

Among the group of respondents it seemed clear that the stronger the negative sanctions the person expected from others—the more he thought he had to lose—the greater the tendency to lump together everyone who was not a proven kindred spirit into the fourth category of potential threats. Those who were most at odds with society reduced our four categories to two, friends and enemies. They had developed a free-floating psychological wariness and duplicity toward everyone who was not cleared as like-minded or tolerant. With several of the informants I had to overcome this suspicious attitude again and again during later conversations, and over a third of the seventy respondents remarked at one time or another that they thought they were talking too much.

Needless to say, such a defensive and suspicious psychological set will have many effects upon a person's daily life. The majority of the respondents felt that they were less open and spontaneous in casual encounters than conventional people, that they couldn't mix as well in conventional settings, and that their inability to be themselves made them somewhat wooden and aloof in public.

The vast majority of the respondents (over eighty percent) were part of some deviant subculture—a circle of intimates—and it was clear that part of the reason was to provide more full and open relationships. A circle of intimates also provided a pool of information to identify local kindred spirits, "alright people," and potential threats. Predictably, the classifying of persons was one of the most frequent topics of conversation. Most of the informants said their local circle of associates was their most frequent channel for becoming acquainted with new kindred spirits, and those who moved about geographically said their subculture was also the best source of information for getting "in" at a new place. A political radical describes the process:

> "I brought a little grass over to Dave's place the other night and talked with him about going to the Bay Area because he'd spent quite a bit of time there last year. He gave me the addresses of a few people where I could probably sleep when I got in and he told me a couple of people who could maybe get me a job. I'd never been there before so he filled me in a little on how it was there for us. Told me a couple of chicks to look up too."

He went on to describe how his last three moves around the country had been helped by such briefings from local intimates. In one case a militant lawyer had written him several letters of introduction and had arranged a place for him to stay for his first month. He, in turn, had later put up another of the lawyer's friends and established him in the local radical scene.

Deviant "connections" are more dangerous than conventional ones. Albert Cohen discusses this problem insightfully in *Delinquent Boys:*

> How does one know whether a gesture . . . will strike a responsive and sympathetic chord in others or whether it will elicit hostility, ridicule and punishment?
>
> The problem is resolved when the innovation is broached in such a manner as to elicit from others reactions suggesting their receptivity; and at the same time the innovation occurs by (stages) so small, tentative, and ambiguous as to permit the actor to retreat if the signs be unfavorable, without having become identified with an unfavorable position.

Perhaps the main device used by deviants to discover allies is casual verbal interchanges. This banter has the built-in escape of "I was only joking" if things get sticky. Such verbal play, common in conventional social life, provides much freedom to explore others and safely make daring suggestions with little fear of consequences. In such encounters deviants often employ language innocuous to conventional people but with signal meanings for fellow deviants or the recruitable. "You're saying several different things in the same breath and watching to see who picks up what."

Developing skill in using such exploratory procedures seems more intuitive than deliberate. It is part of "learning the ropes" in the deviant world and seems to be one of the earmarks of the veteran— part of being cool and in the know.

CONTROL OF COMMUNICATION

Those who engage in activities deemed bad and unacceptable by influential people in their scene must frequently deal with individuals who are not kindred spirits and who embody an unknown degree of threat. The frequency of such contacts with conventionals will vary from person to person according to his activities and his style of life, but no deviant can completely avoid them.

Many situations that seem entirely innocuous to the ordinary person are sources of potential discovery for the deviant. His agenda must include the needs of his conventional and deviant roles. To gain the time and freedom necessary for performing the unacceptable activities, he must practice a deception—the fabricating of a "cover" or, at the very least, the careful omission of part of the truth about himself.

The deviant tries therefore to control all communications directly or tangentially relevant to his unconventional role. How much of the person's total communications with others will be deception varies with the person and his type of deviance. The use of drugs is largely irrelevant to the content of most daily communications unless the person is a dealer or perhaps a psychedelic missionary. A sexual deviance may be carefully separated and almost irrelevant to the rest of someone's daily life or an obsessive preoccupation which colors everything he or she says and does. A mystical worldview or a revolutionary political outlook can pertain to all one's activities or can be almost entirely private.

When communicating with nondeviants, the deviant develops a pattern of behavior that includes the *forms* of conventionality. These forms may only involve monitoring the impressions you give to omit all traces of the unacceptable. But it may require extensive impersonating of a straight person. The use of drugs or a belief in spirits will probably not impinge on the act of buying shoes from a clerk, but a radical's distaste for big business manipulation of fashions or an aberrant sexual interest in the clerk himself well might. The deviant must be alert to and in control of his offhand expressions or his secret will soon be public knowledge. One homosexual respondent said, "When I was home watching television with my folks, I'd catch myself saying, 'There's a good looking guy'."

A black man passing an attractive white girl on a Midwestern street or a radical listening to a presidential candidate or a health food enthusiast watching children eating food with artificial perservatives or a marijuana smoker at a liquor party has much the same problem.

The necessity for such public deceptions forces the deviant to lead a compartmentalized life. However, the careful separation of deviant and conventional activities is seldom completely effective because few social situations are entirely confined to one purpose or one role. Human encounters constantly take surprising turns and so the deviant can never be sure when a situation may spill over into areas relevant to his secret life.

This spillover—the tendency for human interactions to spread out and touch upon a wider range of areas—is an incessant problem for the deviant. One of his most painful and problematic situations is the public denunciation of his secret deviant activity. He will sooner or later be present during discussions of "dope fiends," "queers," "nigger-lovers," "eggheads," "commie-symphs," or whatever other epithets touch upon his private life. Such conversations are usually replete with jibes, stereotyped explanations, belittlements, or at least condescending pity. Such occasions offer three basic possibilities open to the deviant.

(1) He can go along with the general derogatory tone of the discussion by actively contributing to it or by accepting the remarks in silence. But by such acquiescence, he is, in effect, ridiculing and condemning himself, his private memories, his "brothers." It may be very important to remain in good standing with the derogating others because of emotional ties or for more instrumental reasons. But his going along is bought at a high psychological cost. If he comes to take the denunciations seriously he is condemning himself. If he ignores the negative comments he can retain his self respect. But he will almost certainly feel alienated from the denouncers, even if they include a close friend or a parent or his spouse.

Often he will suffer something of both these consequences; he will become more doubtful and defensive about himself and his involvement and attachment to the other people will cool. If such denunciations are frequent, if they come from a preponderance of significant people in his life, and if they are not counterbalanced by strong support from his deviant associates, he will probably come more and more to share their negative opinions and apply them to himself. But he will not be grateful to these critics; in the end he is likely to be bitter about both himself and them.

Several of the respondents reported that they reacted to such situations by deliberately putting the other people on, saying that they got a perverse satisfaction from masquerading as an ultra-condemning square and that their successful concealment in the very midst of those who would reject them if they knew afforded them an emotional thrill. However, the tone and expression of these respondents suggested that this was a "consolation prize," a small satisfaction from an otherwise unpleasant scene.

(2) The deviant may react to such derogations by "leaving the field." He may attempt to psychologically ignore this part of the

conversation or he may try to redirect the discussion into topics more irrelevant to his concealed deviance role. If the remarks are too upsetting he may just break off with these people by getting up and going. If he can't break off with the other people because they are family, coworkers, clients, his leaving may take the form of psychological withdrawal, a wooden playing out of social amenities.

(3) The deviant may react by defending his deviance. This may be an abstract and indirect defense where he chides or condemns the condemners for their prejudice and narrow-mindedness, or where he argues logically for more tolerance. Since at least lip service to tolerance has become widespread and since a fair number of non-deviants do defend the deviant on the basis of their own personal convictions, this is a fairly safe line to take, although it will still direct suspicion to himself. This attacking defense was the most frequent reaction reported by the respondents.

More rarely the defense is confrontation—directly revealing one's own deviance. This may be a defiant self-assertion, a "here I stand," or it may be a confession to significant others. Significantly, a number of informants reported having recurrent dreams and daydreams about such honest self-revelations.

POST-DISCOVERY REACTIONS

One of the main conclusions in a recent research article by John Kitsuse was that public reactions to confrontations and propositions from deviants were far more varied and far less severe than was previously assumed. But Kitsuse only asked the conventional half, not the deviants, about these confrontations. If the public is as gentle as it claimed to be in this study, why is a diffuse suspiciousness and defensiveness so common among the deviant and why do they feel embittered toward conventional society?

The answer seems to be twofold. In the first place, even if most people who learn of someone's deviance are mild and tolerant in their reactions, *the few who are not* force the deviant to be wary. Because it only takes one or at most a few strong negative reactions to spell disaster, the deviant's strategy must be to minimize such losses.

But more important than this are the actual reactions following discovery which the deviants report having experienced. According to these reports many people did indeed react with tolerance and even a measure of support and encouragement upon learning of someone's deviance. Deviants also reported that they were often quite surprised by which persons extended such positive reactions—parents, spouses, ministers, policemen. But these were only minor qualifications to the generally unpleasant consequences of discovery or self-revelation.

Most of the deviants had been through several discovery and self-revelation experiences and they seemed particularly bitter about the results. Although their hearers usually gave verbal expressions of acceptance, they would subsequently disengage themselves from the relationships or attempt to reform the teller or take up a patronizing "you can't help it, you sick thing" attitude.

The respondents said that they most frequently encountered a cooling off of the other persons after the self-revelation. This is, of course, a quite common outcome of conventional interactions; most people go shopping for companionship and turn away from the majority of possibilities after a few exploratory contacts. Several respondents showed that they were aware of this and realized that they did it themselves, but they felt that the withdrawls they had experienced with conventional people were something more. There was a sourness added to the cooling. Some reported that interactions continued but became more sporadic and superficial. The others just didn't get around to calling much any more.

Next to breaking off, the respondents most often encountered efforts to reform them and bring them back into the conventional fold. Health food enthusiasts were invited to meals and tempted with rich desserts and "good solid food, you're looking so thin." Marijuana smokers were pulled into ostensibly philosophical discussions which were loaded with preachments about going astray or living just for kicks, and they were casually handed dire warnings from the Federal Narcotics Bureau. Bohemian poets were offered steady jobs. Intellectuals were enjoined to relax and engage in small talk or canasta. Homosexuals were introduced to charming girls. And Outsiders were given free television sets by relatives.

When relationships weren't simply broken, and even if the others didn't directly engage in reform efforts, the deviants found themselves being pulled into the idea that they had a "problem," as defined by the other people. Others would approach them with new theories and fashionable treatments for their "problem." If the deviant insisted they had no problem except an intolerant society, the objection was not accepted or was merely regarded as another symptom.

Despite these vicissitudes most of the respondents said they would probably continue to reveal their deviance to conventional persons. Why? Because they felt it was the best means for changing public attitudes, and any change was well worth the effort and the risk.

When I mentioned Kitsuse's conclusion to over half the respondents, they agreed that the subjects of the study were probably honest but mistaken—that these conventional people had overestimated their mildness and tolerance in confronting deviants. These deviants, on the other hand, may have overestimated the severity of the reactions they encountered. The truth is probably on both sides. This may be analagous to the Southerner's honest surprise and dismay over the growing racial tensions and strivings. Black unrest has no justification because he and his friends have always "treated their niggers well."

SUMMARY CONCLUSIONS

The facts of a deviant's daily life are determined in large part by the fact that he lives within a disapproving society. His isolation compounds the human problems of procuring and coping. Part of this coping focuses on problems of interaction, and the more a person diverges from the conventional, the more he will tend to classify all those who are not proven allies as threats, and the more likely he is to adopt a public mask.

A deviant's willingness to express and defend his deviance publicly increases with his deviant support and decreases with his dependence upon the conventional public. Just one supportive deviant ally can make the difference.

The greater the relevance of the deviance to the person's total round of interactions with conventionals, the greater the effort involved in keeping the deviance concealed, the more the deviance is likely to be discovered, and the more likely the deviant is to seek an environment more tolerant and supportive.

The deviant is embittered and alienated from society whether he maintains a deception or deviates openly. Either way he is estranged. A homosexual respondent put it this way:

> "When I was younger I went through these soulful confessions and I lost more friends that way. Folks too. Now I go to the john right alongside the rest of the men.

I play it cool and I've pulled together a good life for myself. Except when I look in the mirror and think, 'You fucking queer'."

The furtiveness of the deviant is more understandable when we realize that, to pursue his deviant activities, he must continually *trust* both the willingness and the competence of a fairly large number of people to keep his secret. Even if he only interacts cautiously with one or two members of the local underground, at least several others are likely to know about him in a general way. The deviant somewhat depends upon all those who know about him and since he never can be certain who will cop out, gossip, or talk under police pressure, he is continually prey to a diffuse sense of uneasiness which may alienate him from an already alienated group.

CHAPTER SEVEN

DEVIANT

SUBCULTURES

In response to society's disapproval and harassment deviants usually hand together with others in the same plight. Beyond the ties of similar interests and views which lie at the base of most human associations, deviants find that establishing fairly stable relationships with other deviants does much to ease procurement and coping problems and to provide a more stable and reliable source of direct support and interaction. In these indirect ways, society's condemnation "creates" the deviant subculture. When disapproval eases, the "subculture" may attenuate or even disintegrate. For example, the present subculture of users is something like the subculture of alcohol drinkers during Prohibition.

"Deviant subculture" is a stripped-down scientific abstraction for a very real and concrete thing—most deviants live in connection with other deviants and "sympathizers," even if this be only half a dozen people in a little Midwestern town. And such subcultures evolve their own little communities or social worlds, each with its own local myths (the county attorney goes easy with us cause he's an old head himself), its own legendary heroes (remember Max—what a crazy one he was), its own honorary members (Blaine the druggist or Sophie at the cafe), its own scale of reputations (Garth's all right, he's just a little slow about some things), and its own social routine (probably see you at the Totem later on tonight).

The term is useful because it points to something important; deviants tend to get together. There are deviant traditions and ideologies, deviant prestige systems, commitment and conformity to deviant codes, deviant recruitment and missionary work, and deviant utopian dreams.

But the social scientists have also been taken in by their own word game. My conclusion from field research with two rural delinquent gangs, a health food coterie, two mystic groups, several beatnik and hippie groups, and various student fringe groups is that "deviant subcultures" are in actuality far from the tightly-knit, highly cohesive, clearly structured entities they are pictured to be in social science literature, police records, or the press. These misconceptions are projected onto what, in reality, is usually no more than a bunch of people with ever-shifting, overlapping relationships. Such groups are amorphous and quite unstable through time. Goals and purposes, moral codes, and even memberships are often only semi-conscious. Commitment and loyalties to the group wax and wane, and they are seldom dependable. I recall the remark of a mischievous teenager in Cedar Rapids, Iowa: "I had no idea I belonged to a delinquent gang until the cops told me."

The notion of "deviant subculture," therefore, is itself a stereotype which is partly true but also false in several important respects. Lewis Yablonsky's concept, "near-group"—a collectivity of people whose degree of cohesion and organization falls somewhere between a mob and a true group—applies, I think, far more accurately to the realities of deviants associating together. There are shared understandings among the participants, but their interpersonal relations are also shot through with many misunderstandings and miscarried intentions. Any "organization" is usually informal, uncrystallized and unstable beyond a few weeks.

With a few notable exceptions, such as the Hell's Angels, the commitment of the participants to one another and to the group as a whole is tenuous and half-hearted. For individual "members" it varies. On one occasion it may be an intense brotherhood; on the next the individuals may be willing to sell each other out to save themselves or to obtain some small personal gain. (Sometimes this personal gain may be no more than the undivided attention of a reporter or a bit of flattery from an investigator.)

Membership itself is often vague, and the line between "us" and "them" wavers and changes. The dichotomy of members and non-members is oversimple; usually a few core members are unequivocally committed, a larger circle of part-time members drift back and forth between conventionality and deviance, and an even larger circle are only tangentially acquainted or involved. These last two circles, and sometimes even the few at the core, constantly move in and out of the subculture. They are occupied with a variety of conventional as well as deviant activities and commitments. Rather than being the essential part of their lives, the deviance may be only a casual weekend thing or the result of an occasional spree.

The supposed members are often not very clear in their own minds on what the group is about, who else is in it, what it attempts to accomplish. And different members will give conflicting views on these matters.

Even leadership and other designations of functions are vague and constantly changing. Factionalism and incessant internal shifts in personal status are the rule rather than the exception. Internal statuses tend to be negotiated and temporary, so control of individual members by the group isn't really all that extensive.

These vagaries are why drug use or black radicalism or homo-sexuality can't be eradicated by dealing with the supposed leaders. There are eminent people in these and similar fringe movements but there is no "head to lop off." A teacher in one of the depressed schools of Wichita, Kansas, exclaimed after the assasination of Martin Luther King, "Good, that'll be the end of all this trouble and unrest." I could only feel sorry for her on various counts.

We mustn't, however, err in the opposite direction by suggesting that the whole subculture notion is false. A deviant's closer associates are statistically most likely to be other fringe people. There are discernible deviant social worlds, partially insulated and estranged from the society at large, each with its subterranean traditions, its own literature and slang, its own beliefs and ways of looking at things. All these things exist but in varying degrees, not as hard and fast characteristics.

The ambivalence of the participants is the main thing that keeps deviant subcultures from becoming more solid. Most members are of two minds about deviating and most of them still have many conventional commitments. My observations suggest that the vast majority of deviants inhabit dual worlds of deviance/conventionality and when things aren't going well in the one they turn to the other. They vacillate between the two as situations and opportunities shift. This is essentially what David Matza found in his study of delinquent gangs.

A visible deviant group is the symptom and surface of some larger and more widespread fringe drift within the society. The Women's Christian Temperance Union, for instance, was only the organized spearhead of a Prohibition backlash against the perceived moral decline of urbanism—the Prohibition mood was felt by far more people than were members of this organization, and it spread beyond a fight against liquor into action against illicit drugs, sex, political liberalism and so on. Delinquent gangs were only the more spectacular aspects of the failure of the huge metropolis to take human care of its inhabitants. The hippies are only the more far out examples of the pervasive unrest and disillusionment of a whole generation of youth with standard-brand America. And the Black Panthers are but a more vocal and visible swell on the surface of a deep militant thrust of twenty million blacks for a place in the sun.

Sometimes changes in these fringe drifts will leave particular deviant groups aground to flounder and finally expire for lack of underlying support. This seems to be the fate of the old Marxist radicals in the United States; younger radicals have gone beyond Communism as well as capitalism. Also the delinquent tough is coming to seem more and more an anachronism even to other estranged youths who are now looking to hippie and post-hippie models. Herbert Blumer and his associates, for example, found among Bay Area adolescents a steady decline in the prestige of such once-admired delinquent gangs.

More often there is a number of different delinquent groups expressing a range of different positions in the fringe drift. Most such groups are more fleeting and unstable than the underlying deviant subcultural drift that spawned them. Wife-swapping clubs, sexual freedom leagues, the Keristans are only facets of the erotic revolution in our time.

Societal condemnation gives powerful support to the creation and continuation of these deviant groups. Even when the members don't altogether agree with or even like each other they are thrown together because they may have nowhere else to turn for help and support. But just about everything else is against them. Unlike conventional associations, deviant groups must solve their internal conflicts and problems without any supports from the larger society; they must solve their own squabbles in the face of many impediments. External pressure can crush a group as well as solidify it, as the example of the black man and his white girlfriend in the last chapter demonstrated.

With so many against them, externally and internally, how can deviant groups hold together and "make it"? The following case history gives some explanation.

MAINTAINING DEVIANT BELIEFS: THE ESPERS

This case study explores the belief system shared by a small group of mystics to discover how the members maintain their divergent beliefs in the face of a disbelieving larger society. I gathered the data through participant observation, lengthy interviews with a prominent member of the group, and a number of shorter interviews with other members. I also examined pamphlets and newsletters of the organization and drew upon observations from other fringe groups to round out the conclusions.

The group, which we'll call Esper, is headquartered in a semi-isolated mountainous area of Georgia. The group picked their locale partly for its seclusion and partly for the natural protection it would afford in the event of a nuclear war. Several members had sold their businesses and properties in other locations to settle here permanently. The buildings and grounds are extensive, including housing for perhaps two hundred people, ample garden space, springs, and orchards. (It was an abandoned resort.)

Several other fringe groups who share many beliefs about the world with the Espers are located within a few miles of the camp, and there are many institutional and informal ties with these other groups. Multiple membership is rare, the ties seem to result from shared beliefs, admiration of the same fringe heroes, a common fringe literature and folklore. But the strongest bond among the groups seems to be a shared attitude of suspicion and benevolent contempt toward the society at large and its "unenlightened" followers.

I was unable to get exact figures on the size of membership of Esper. As is almost always the case with fringe groups, there was a tendency to exaggerate its actual size into the thousands. The more sober estimates, which were in line with my own observations, clustered around fifty full members and perhaps a hundred marginal associates. About twenty-five of these lived in or near the headquarters and most of the rest lived within a day or two's drive. There were over three hundred subscribers to the Esper monthly newsletter; subscription price was five dollars per year. Membership dues were thirty dollars initiation fee and five dollars per year thereafter. The two main sources of income for the organization and its salaried members were fees for the use of cabins, boats, etc., and fees for training in psychic powers. Individual members made other monies through such arts as faith-healing, the practice of "natural medicine," and readings of psyches through photographs and signatures.

At this point you might wonder about the possibility of fraud, the cynical manipulation of the membership by a few individuals for financial gain. I sought evidence for this possibility but concluded that there was no deliberate hoaxing involved. A number of members did earn their living through mystic work but their earnings would be judged barely above subsistence level by ordinary American standards. The Elmer Gantry type was conspicuously absent; the leaders seemed to believe firmly in what they were doing and did it without fanfare.

Members ranged in age from fourteen into the seventies and included roughly as many women as men. In some cases couples or entire families were members, in other cases only one or two individuals from a family would belong.

The formal education level of the group seemed average at best. However the group was unmistakably far above average in one respect—the amount and variety of reading they did. Their reading included fringe literature, such as books and magazines on flying saucers, hypnotism, mythology, health food and herb medicine, mysticism and occultism, science fiction, the writings of Mary Baker Eddy, Pak Subud, J. B. Rhine, and exposes of the larger society.

Many of the members were also voracious readers of conventional magazines, paperback books, and serious literature.

Most members had atypical life-histories. These included the early loss of one or both parents, bizarre relationships with parents, parents who were themselves fringe, abnormal schooling and work-histories. But I don't think the members were there because they had "failed" in ordinary society, as has sometimes been suggested about members of deviant subcultures.

Such unusual backgrounds, combined with an unusual breadth of reading, produced broad, though unsystematic, knowledge about the world. Among Espers and similar fringe groups you may easily meet individuals acquainted with the Sanskrit poets, Norse mythology, medieval painting, or German Idealist philosophy. However, they tend not to be "cultured" in the sense of having a standard scholarship in the humanities. A member might not know who Woodrow Wilson or the governor of his state was. Espers also seem to lack the rigor or critical ability associated with formal education. They ignored or didn't grasp the conventional forms for the reliability of sources and logical argument. At the same time, they possessed an inquiring attitude and an openness of mind that would have delighted Bacon.

Espers interpret happenings in ways that would seem fantastic to the layman. Their view of human nature echoes the Eastern religious conception that Man is a creature distracted and blinded by the sensory pageant of external events, who is largely asleep and unaware of his true makeup or potentialities. Most of man's spiritual life goes on independently from the conscious individual and largely without his awareness unless he is enlightened. The Esper world is peopled with disembodied spirits, good and bad, and with all the psychic powers, at least in rudimentary form, and these may be cultivated and trained by instruction from those who have already reached awareness. Telepathy, clairvoyance, telekinesis, communication with spirits, reincarnation, mystical intuition, dowsing, manipulating events through faith and magical procedures *are real and everyday occurrences to the Espers and similar groups*. These groups are adamant in their disagreement with the version of reality presented in conventional scientific and historical writings. They see the ordinary citizen as a sleepwalker, a superstition-ridden primitive. Mystic enlightenment is considered a more valid source of knowledge, and especially understanding, than our culture-bound commonsense and scientific method.

Some readers may wonder how individuals can continue to accept or live by such a "crazy" belief system. Anyone who has grown up to accept conventional American culture might find it incredible that people could believe such weird things in the face of so much contrary evidence. But as we explore some of the processes involved in confirming and maintaining Esper beliefs, it will become more and more apparent that *all* belief systems, including the conventional American view of things, are to some extent arbitrary and that the same mechanisms are employed in maintaining them. The concept of the "self-fulfilling prophecy," first advanced by W. I. Thomas, is particularly useful in our exploration.

First, as Jerome Bruner has shown, we all tend to select and pay attention to only that part of the total influx of incoming sense perceptions that fits in with our own expectations. This seeing only what we expect to see may even involve the active supplying of perceptions which are not really there, as in the case of geometric illusions. But more important in confirming a belief is the fact that most situations are only semi-structured so that an individual has some freedom in structuring them to come "true."

Examples may clarify these points. I was sitting in a coffee shop with my main Esper informant when a young woman sat down at a table beside us. Her hair was a neutral brown and short-cut, her features angular, and her hands long and thin. The most striking aspect of her physical appearance was the bright shade of her lipstick and matching nail polish. My informant leaned forward with some agitation and told me in a low voice that she was a hunting demon who drained men of their psychic energy and left them empty hulks. Her true nature was reflected in her psychic aura which he could plainly read. His distress seemed genuine as he asked me to extend psychic protection over him because he felt "no match for her power."

A few minutes later a young man joined her at the table and we were able to overhear their conversation. They talked for perhaps three-quarters of an hour before leaving, and the girl's conversation covered a wide variety of attitudes about many different subjects. But after they had gone, my informant cited, as corroboration of his judgment, only those statements which might be construed as reflecting a grasping, manipulative attitude toward the world. Other statements which expressed coquettishness, admiration for other people, a simple appreciation of music, and sympathy for the plight of the American black and so on were entirely neglected by the Esper. (I'm not ruling out the possibility that she *was* a hunting demon.)

The second aspect of the self-fulfilling prophecy is more subtle than selective attention but common with Espers and other fringe groups as well as among conventional people in defending their views. It might be described by the following paradigm:

A. A person makes some inference about another.

B. The person acts toward the other on the basis of this judgment.

C. The other makes inferences about the person on the basis of his actions.

D. The other reacts toward the person on the basis of his inference.

E. Thus the person's inferences about the other tend to be confirmed by the other's reactions.

This paradigm is merely a slight modification of many social psychological theories of the interpersonal process, but its self-fulfilling aspects are usually missed. When a situation is rigidly structured the possibilities for such self-fulfilling confirmations will, of course, be quite limited. It would be difficult to interpret and confirm a minister's actions at a funeral as a sexual advance, for example. But all situations are to some extent flexible so that the participants always have at least some freedom in defining them and affecting their outcomes.

For example, my informant rented a room for several days from a middle-aged woman. After seeing her only briefly, and before he had spoken with her, he "intuited" that she was a warm accepting woman full of psychic strength and goodness. When he first talked with her a couple hours later, his manner was far more friendly and "turned on" than usual. He showed interest in her collection of antiques, inquired about her children and how she had passed on her warm spirit to them, and ended by saying he sensed she was a wonderful person and he wanted to rent from her partly because they would have more chances to talk together. During the next few days, I had a chance to ask other tenants and neighbors about the landlady. They described a caustic gossiper who was unusually strict about tenants' use of electricity, property, and grounds. Her attitude toward me was grudging and taciturn. But she responded graciously to my informant's open friendliness. She sought him out to chat with on several occasions, she inquired if there was enough light in him room for late reading and supplied him with an extra table lamp, etc. *In her behavior toward him,* my informant's intuition certainly came true.

It seems a safe generalization that nobody can continue to maintain beliefs if a large amount of contradicting evidence is *perceived.* This is why the conventional person finds it so difficult to see how fringers can believe in "all that crazy stuff" (or why the Russian people are so easily "duped" by Communist propaganda). Where is their "common sense," he asks. But the point is that "common sense" varies widely and arbitrarily from group to group.

Extending some ideas developed by Milton Rokeach and his associates, we may say that groups and cultures build up belief systems that paint a fairly coherent and consistent picture of the world. But how accurately do these portraits represent the "real world"? Are some belief systems more accurate than others? And how can we compare their accuracy since each belief system gathers and sifts its own confirming evidence? Can we establish that the Espers are wrong and the *Reader's Digest* (or *Ramparts* or *Scientific American)* is right?

Throughout human history judgments about which belief systems are true have been made ethnocentrically, on the basis of the judge's own beliefs. The groups with the most power have traditionally foisted their beliefs upon weaker groups at the point of a bayonet and that was about the extent of the debate—until the balance of power between the groups shifted again.

In the popular mind, science is thought to be able to evaluate objectively the truth of beliefs about reality. But this popular notion is untrue, as some of the most eminent scientists have themselves said. And as a matter of fact, modern physics has advanced to the point that the field has demolished virtually all its own theories. In the behavioral sciences, we still know so little that almost no assertions about human beings, including those of the Espers, can be disproven conclusively.

To put it another way, confirming evidence for particular beliefs about reality is sought and *found* because most situations are ambiguous enough to allow them to be *interpreted* in various ways. We needn't bring in fringe groups as examples, since this is a mechanism used by all people in maintaining their beliefs. For instance, any Communist offer for disarmament is automatically interpreted as a propaganda move by the American government and press. Lack of information makes this interpretation possible whether or not it accurately reflects the real motives of the Communist governments. And our hostility is the reason for our lack of information about them. In fact, it is difficult to imagine a Communist action that Americans would accept as an honest move for peace. Of course, the Communists interpret our actions in a similar way.

It is difficult to break into this circle of confirmation—to change the views of a person who is entrenched in a particular belief system—because situations are *defined* and *interpreted* by the very notions that a critic wants to discredit. For instance, Espers define man as a spiritual being possessing a psychic aura. By reading these auras, Espers can make certain inferences about peoples' spiritual characters. You can't demonstrate to Espers that individuals do not have psychic auras. In fact, ironically modern science, with its sensitive devices for measuring organic electrical fields, has given scientific support to this Esper conviction. Fringe group members often cite such scientific evidence in support of their claims, although the scientific findings are broadly interpreted and selectively quoted.

A further means by which Espers are able to keep their beliefs is through association and identification with other Espers on the one hand, and relative isolation from non-Espers on the other. As an interacting group, Espers provide support for the individual member in his view of the world. As many deviants have put it, they feel they can be themselves only with kindred fringers. Members feel "at home" because they share a common language with which they can communicate their views and problems with others who share their meanings.

Communication within the group provides further confirming evidence for the belief system. For example, several Espers will be able to "read" someone's psychic aura, and, although they might quibble over details of one another's reading, they all "see" the aura. Of course this sort of confirmation through consensus among intimates isn't confined to deviant groups. A psychiatric staff reaches agreement that a patient is "paranoid schizophrenic" because their similar educations train them to "see" the same symptoms. Or a group of similarly trained sociologists "percieve" that modern man is alienated. Or a group of like-minded senators can clearly "see" that an increased military budget is more important than foreign aid.

In almost all groups, deviant or conventional, a person's judgments about reality are not really accepted until he has been certified as successfully socialized into the group, until he has learned the processes for arriving at the "right" answers. You can't pass your medical boards by prescribing health foods and you can't keep a ministry post by debunking the faith. By this process of "screening" who they'll listen to or take seriously, Espers, and all groups, insulate themselves to a great extent from really contrary opinions. And this provides the rationale for saying that those who disagree are not competent to judge. Thus the Espers explained that the ordinary man couldn't read psychic auras because he hadn't been trained to do so and because he was entirely out of touch with his own Spiritual Self.

Several times I saw Espers apply this rationale in dealing with non-Espers. Conventional people who were tolerant toward Esper views were, in every case I observed, judged to be psychic themselves. Those who were indifferent or openly scornful were judged to be either hopelessly asleep or psychic but evil. The Espers seemed to be entirely unaware of this latent criterion for judging non-Espers.

Finally, Espers and similar fringe groups are aided in maintaining their unconventional beliefs by the ambivalence of the larger society toward them. In our culture, a mystical worldview is a well established counter-theme to our dominant materialism and pragmatism. In describing Puerto Rican spiritualism Rogler and Hollingshead noted, "If you ever talk to a Puerto Rican who says he doesn't believe in Spirits, you know what that means? It means you haven't talked to him long enough." I think the same could be said for most Americans. Tales of psychic happenings and of individuals gifted with extrasensory perception are widely, although informally, told in our society. And a large number of Americans have been convined at one time or another that "there is something to them." Almost everyone has an aunt who answers the phone before it rings or a grandmother who senses when her children are in trouble. Such widespread ambivalence tends to soften the disbelief and rejection by the conventional person when interacting with the mystic. I have questioned many conventional people on their attitudes toward Espers and similar groups and the most frequent reply has been that, although they're a bit "crackpot" there well may be something in their notions.

Fringe group members are usually keenly aware of the fact that the larger society disagrees with their view of reality. They tend to adopt a defensive judgment of the layman as unenlightened, unless he shows himself otherwise. This judgment makes it easier for the fringe group member to disregard the rejection or derision of the unbeliever. Either way his own views are confirmed.

CHANGING DEVIANT BEHAVIOR

How can such beliefs be changed? Punishment or the threat of it can make someone keep quiet or become more careful or stop doing something, at least until the threat diminishes, but it can't change the mind of a delinquent boy, a homosexual, or an Esper. For example, the evidence suggests that the most our jails teach prisoners is to be more cool in the future.

Reasoning usually doesn't work because the beliefs are quite frequently subconscious. Also the reasoning processes you're likely to use are yours, not theirs. If you know and grant their "premises" you can sometimes argue deductively that some of their notions are incompatible with others, or perhaps that their conclusions don't follow. Thus, you can suggest to hippies that heroin is uncool because it turns you off instead of on. And hippies can argue convincingly with straight people that Christians are supposed to practice peace.

Just because two different beliefs within a system are in conflict, however, doesn't mean that the believers will relinquish one of them. The human mind seems perfectly capable of simultaneously embracing two or more disparate notions—or of creatively arguing away the apparent disparity. For example, Espers believe that a person's future is in his own hands, but they also believe that "awakened" people can forsee an inevitable future (precognition). When I pointed this out it seemed to trouble the Espers not at all. (This inconsistency should have a familiar ring to social scientists.)

You can sometimes point out events in the "real world" which challenge part of a belief system, deviant or otherwise. The main difficulty here is that both you and the believer must have some minimum common agreement about "reality." Everyone must, of course, make some concessions to objective reality or he will not survive. Whatever your beliefs, some beaches do have riptides. Methadrine does do massive damage to the central nervous system, and nuclear missles can obliterate whole populations. As anthropologist

Clyde Kluckhohn pointed out, no culture can survive long if its beliefs are too far out of line with "the facts of nature."

But here again we must be very cautious lest we ethnocentrically assume that our own group's views are the necessary and correct orientations toward reality. When adversaries from divergent belief systems confront one another, each is likely to feel that the other is "out of touch with reality." Espers believe that some people can levitate themselves over buildings or project their astral bodies through space, and I have seen Espers and non-Espers each walk away smiling contemptuously at the other after discussing these possibilities. Similarly, I have seen many parents and their children turn away from each other, each feeling that the other has lost track of reality.

If there is minimum agreement among the divergent parties about what goes on in the real world, each can question the other's beliefs by referring to these common realities. For instance, Espers believe in reincarnation and they also will acknowledge the fact that the human and animal population of the world is increasing. Juxtaposing these two beliefs, I asked several Espers where more souls for the greater number of living bodies come from. The Espers recognized the inconsistency and admitted they could give no answer. My main informant became so interested in the question he read books on Eastern religions and asked a good many of the other Espers what they thought. (I may have thus unwittingly started a chain of events that will produce innovations in the Esper belief system.)

This "referral to the facts" is commonly held up as the mainstay of persuasive conversation. But my observations of many encounters between members of divergent subcultures has led me to think we often overestimate the utility of such "reasonable debates." Conferences between delinquents and authorities, between blacks and whites, between hippies and straights, between youths and parents follow a pattern: sitting down together with mixed intentions, talking past one another for awhile, becoming more defensive and antagonistic toward one another, and leaving with the feeling that really communicating with the other party is a hopeless task. George Wallace and Robert Kennedy might have agreed that a lightbulb is a lightbulb, but they didn't really live in the same world. A minimum of consensus over some empirical facts isn't necessarily enough to serve as a real communications bridge.

Changing someone's belief is most likely when he is already ambivalent. We noted earlier that deviants are ambivalent in varying degrees about their divergent attitudes and activities, so the potential for "reaching them" is there. This is the other side of the point already made that all conventional people are, in varying degrees, seduceable into deviance.

Deviant belief systems do change and evolve with time. They are more amorphous and fluctuating than we usually assume, just as the groups holding them are more amorphous and fluctuating than most people realize. Today's Black Panther or hippie or homosexual or mystic may think and feel significantly different than he did even a year ago. This summer's New York City delinquent or Los Angeles hipster can be expected to look, act, and think differently than last summer's, although there are many continuities, resemblances, and traditions upheld.

These changes in deviant beliefs are internal evolutions coupled with adjustments to changes in conditions external to the group. The mechanisms involved are ill-understood, but the underlying point is clear. Deviant subcultures have a natural history just as do total societies.

One other point must be made about confirming or challenging beliefs through evidence and reason. Since beliefs comingle thought and emotion and rest ultimately on untestable value-premises they resemble ideologies or religious convictions more than hypotheses which can be proven or disproven. A fairly large part of every belief system is therefore beyond the challenge of empirical events and is susceptible only to the persuasion of competing value-premises.

In the movement back and forth between deviant and conventional subcultures, people are converted more than convinced. People turn to pot because they find it more fun than liquor; people have illicit sexual adventures because they find them more satisfying than abstinence; people join the fringes of society for the adventure of it and because it fills some vacuum within themselves. The beliefs and the subcultures often come afterwards, not first.

CHAPTER EIGHT

OFFICIALS

AND CULPRITS

Every social world, whether it be a total institution, such as a prison, partially closed, such as a liberal arts college, or relatively open, such as an urban neighborhood, has a number of basic characteristics which set the basis for the relationship between authorities and rule-breakers. Within the milieu processes are occurring as means toward achieving certain ends, such as the custody and rehabilitation of convicts, the education and "culling" of students for the larger society, the maintenance of what is locally considered as the good life, or the production of goods and services. There is also a population directly and indirectly involved in these processes. These people may be there willingly, unwillingly, or simply through the historical accidents of placement. There is a body of rules, both official and unofficial, which applies to the populace engaged in these processes. And there is a group of authorities or officials who supervise the ongoing processes by applying, interpreting, and sometimes modifying these rules upon this population. In addition, publics outside the milieu are concerned with the course of its internal workings and productions. For every social setting there are usually several of these interested, external publics—parents and alumni, the press, federal, state, and local governments, tourists, moral reform groups, adjacent neighborhoods, other institutions, and the general public.

The authorities within the social setting are faced with a complex job, a job far more complicated and difficult than any official job description. Officials must see that the ongoing processes are maintained at some minimally satisfactory level and they are often expected to increase efficiency—to care for more patients or convicts, graduate more students, or keep more citizens peaceful. They must successfully procure what they need for this maintenance and enhancement. They must regulate the population in such a way that the processes continue, the populace is not sparked to rebellion, and those publics concerned with morality are mollified. And they must maintain and if possible improve the public image of the institution or area, in competition with the public relations efforts of other areas. The official is responsive to his external publics, at least in the sense that he must negotiate their noninterference. He is usually dependent on some external publics for his resources, and some of these publics will, in a sense, be his supervisors. To fully understand the deviant, we must understand the situation of the officials who confront and deal with him.

If the actual aims of the milieu are different than the officially stated goals, or if the processes have other functions which cannot be made public, or if the various external publics who influence the milieu have conflicting ideas about what should be going on, the jobs of officials are further complicated. *And all of these complicating factors usually exist.*

The official's main way of resolving these difficulties and balancing the accompanying cross-pressures is to judiciously interpret and apply the host of rules at his disposal. He is literally a rule-er in his own domain. These rules can be multitudinous, including constitutions and charters, official regulations, bylaws, well-established precedents, rituals, informal understandings, and the rules of external agencies that are binding upon the milieu. (For example, state universities or prisons are not supposed to violate federal laws.) Additionally, most officials can, and are expected to, make new rules and establish new operating procedures. So "the rules" include far more than the printed book of regulations handed to the new convict, student, or recruit.

The rank and file of large organizations view those in authority with a mixture of suspicion, rebelliousness, and respect. Authorities always try to promote loyalty and subservience to the milieu and its officials. But such efforts are only partly successful. So authority must combine education with reward and punishment. *Hence, officials are usually stereotyped by the rank and file as "watchdogs" who must be dealt with carefully and circumspectly, even when they are friendly.* This means, among other things, that there is always some social and psychological distance between officials and their populations.

Such bodies of rules exist to maintain order and continuity within the social setting and facilitate its processes. However, you can never take it for granted that the rules do, in fact, serve these purposes. The rules have a variable impact; they may facilitate the social processes, they may be irrelevant to them, or they may actually impede them. If conditions have changed significantly since the rules were first formulated, or if the rules have been imposed "from above" by special-interest external publics, or if the actual aims diverge very much from the officially stated goals, the existing rules will be at least somewhat inconvenient to both authorities and populace. Officials and populace together often find that they must cooperatively engage in a collective duplicity which throws up a facade of rule-adherence but which actually bends the rules so that the processes can be effectively carried out. This often includes a semi-deliberate cutoff of information flow both ways between the officials and the population. For example, officials usually don't inquire too closely into the working procedures of their subordinates as long as things go fairly well. And police leave most of the people and houses on their beat alone as long as there is no public disturbance.

In most circumstances, the processes take priority over the rules because if the processes go wrong the milieu literally breaks up and leaves everyone adrift. The disruption causes internal turmoil, brings interference from the external publics, and discredits the officials in charge. If the processes go well officials almost always redeem themselves even amid widespread and obvious rule-infractions. But if the social setting breaks down the official has clearly failed in his role as supervisor, even if all the rules have been upheld. Most officials know these "facts of life" and act accordingly.

The population too is always ambivalent toward the body of rules. Even when "membership" in the social setting is entirely voluntary (and is this ever really the case?) that setting will seldom if ever command the unequivocal loyalty of its population. Even when it does, the loyalty is usually to the milieu as a whole and its goals. So the "loyal people" too may be motivated to break the rules that seem detrimental to the whole. In order for there to be perfect loyalty and compliance with the body of rules, the population would have to be perfectly "programmed" to embrace the rules and goals, there would have to be a perfect meshing between rules and goals, and a perfect integration of all the elements in this system. It would also require that the milieu was perfectly self-contained and self-sufficient, without dependence upon, interference from, or loyalties to external forces. Of course none of these conditions exists in the real world.

Existing institutions, organizations, and settings make a quite different picture. The authorities and the population vacillate between uneasy alliance and open conflict. There is at least some divergence between the rules and the aims, and often within the rules between official regulations and unwritten procedures. The various aims of the social processes are usually less than entirely compatible. For example, the official aim of juvenile detention halls is usually rehabilitation, but their actual function is mainly custody and punishment. The influences of the various external publics are usually in conflict with one another and with at least some aims of the milieu, especially the unofficial ones. At least some of the population will be attached to values and standards that diverge from those prevailing in the milieu. And the officials may be led to countenance, or even encourage, widespread infractions of the rules.

To some readers this portrait might seem to be an undue exaggeration of the conflict and disruptive facets of social settings—a biased portrait that neglects the integrated, smooth-running side of things. Aren't the turmoils smaller and mostly due to "outside agitators"?

I suggest that the above portrait seems exaggerated only because of the current fashion of presenting peaceful facades by publicly overstating the smooth-running and harmonious aspects of a situation. To test my contention ask yourself two questions. First, have you ever gotten "inside" any organization, institution, or complex situation without finding a nest of conflicts of interests, clique competitions, ambiguities, irrationalities, pluralistic ignorances, subversions, and public relations duplicities toward the external public and toward some of its own people? Second, haven't you emerged from a personal turmoil, a sad consideration of your current lot, a family quarrel, or a subversive intent and answered the question "How are you?" with "Oh, just fine"? Our personal and organizational "front," so insightfully discussed by Erving Goffman, shouldn't be mistaken for the realities it is designed to cover.

A large proportion of any population routinely breaks some rules, and most of the insiders, including the authorities, know or sense this. The newcomer to the institution, organization or social scene must "learn the ropes" if he is to survive and prosper. He must learn just which kinds and degrees of those infractions are unofficially acceptable and which are likely to be judged clearly out-of-bounds. There is, however, always some no man's land between acceptable and unacceptable rule-bending. And there is always a certain risk involved in following courses of action that skirt these mobile boundaries. Ironically, as we'll see there is also a certain risk in following the letter of the rules. Whatever course you follow has a certain risk inherent in being actively involved in any milieu.

Seasoned officials ignore or make only mildly disapproving gestures toward moderate infractions. They act in their full-dress official capacity infrequently and sporadically, not routinely. New officials feel many and diverse pressures to adopt such a loose-reined style, and they frequently find their careers impeded or even destroyed if they don't. Rule-bound, ultra-moralistic officials inconvenience and embarrass both their superiors and their subordinates. Consequently they are often stopped in mid-career.

Even when an infraction is clearly out of bounds, officials will, for a variety of reasons, usually take some course of action against the culprit that falls far short of their full official powers. Perhaps the main reason is that the official's time and resources are always limited. Dealing with infractions eats up already overtaxed effort and resources. Even fanatic officials can deal only with a fraction of the culprits in their population. Some of the most far-reaching decisions authorities make are which rules and goals to emphasize and which to neglect.

The official's selective enforcement is partly determined by internal and external pressures and is partly a matter of his own feelings. Influential publics may pressure him to pay special attention to some rules, or he may find that some rules are crucial to social processes. Some officials will use their offices to enforce the rules they consider morally right. For this reason especially, a change in officials usually means a change in the rules enforced.

The official may refrain from dealing with an infraction also because he is convinced that the culprit is performing important services for the ongoing social processes and their aims. If he feels that full official retribution would curtail these services he may ignore the culprit and he may even actively "cover" for him.

Not infrequently the reverse occurs. A minor infraction becomes the pretext for dismissing or failing to promote someone who is disapproved of on other grounds. Since virtually everyone can be found guilty of some infractions, the official has a ready means for dealing with someone deemed unsuitable or someone he and his publics disapprove of. California officials have, for example, harassed hippie communes and psychedelic shops by rigorously enforcing obscure ordinances. A bearded, bell-wearing youth was arrested before my eyes on a southern California beach for "playing a musical instrument in public without a license."

Officials also refrain from full rule-enforcement if it would attract unwanted attention from some of the external publics. The publicity resulting from such a public "scandal" might well disrupt the milieu and perhaps their own comfortable position within it. For example, as long as sexual liaisons and drug connections on campuses remain quiet and within bounds, administrators tend to make only token gestures of enforcement because the "full story" would embarrass. They can't stamp out such practices by fully enforcing official university regulations without risking a nationwide scandal.

However, if the official wishes such public attention because of personal ambitions, moral reasons, or because of loyalties to external publics, he may fully enforce rules which no one has been taking seriously. For instance, a young district attorney in a Midwestern city, who admitted having political ambitions, rounded up a "ring of homosexuals" and won a higher political office with the help of the favorable publicity. The legal grounds for the round-up were flimsy; the courts handed the group of twenty-six over to the state psychiatric board who immediately released them without action. In another recent example a state attorney general running for governor launched a newsstand cleanup campaign against the smaller publishers of girlie magazines and erotic books, even though recent obscenity trial decisions established that he had no legal grounds for doing so. He immediately dropped the purity plank when he won the state primaries.

Officials may also refrain from full rule-enforcement where they feel the rules are grossly unrealistic. Most local, state, and national governments, for example, have rules on the books which are not taken seriously by anyone—laws against kissing in public or rules that every faculty advisor must confer once a semester will each of his student advisees. Other rules are largely for public display, such as the regulations against sexual intimacies among undergraduate students at major universities or the laws against selling cigarettes to minors. There are other rules which are taken more seriously but which are seldom fully enforced because the mandatory punishments are too harsh. Examples of these are regulations calling for the automatic court-martial of AWOL military personnel, expulsion of students caught cheating, and long prison sentences for first offenders caught smoking marijuana.

Again there are situations in which the reverse occurs; someone is fully punished for doing no more than what a large number of other people are doing. Such "victims" may be sacrificed for a show of enforcement to external publics or for an official's own personal reasons.

Even if the official feels that the rules are just and realistic, he may "save" rather than destroy the culprits for humanitarian reasons or because the culprit is a promising soldier, graduate, citizen, etc. The official knows, perhaps better than the culprit, that blacklisting can have tough, long-term effects. So if there is any doubt about guilt, or if there are extenuating circumstances, the official will often hesitate to take drastic action. Officers hesitate to bring charges against those under their command when conviction means a firing squad. And seasoned attorneys say the stiffer a sentence will be, the more reluctant juries are to convict.

Finally, the official may refrain from full rule-enforcement because he fears retribution from the population under him. No population is entirely defenseless against its officials, although the balance of power certainly favors the authorities. The populace can effectively sabotage, by massive passive resistance, the official's efforts, embarrass him publicly, spoil his record, and destroy his career. In more extreme cases there are procedures to remove him from office, although law and tradition favor the official in such contests. And as a last resort, officials can always be killed. Many a revolutionary leader has been saved from execution because the authorities in charge knew full well that there were friends in the hills (or the ghettos) who would take revenge.

At least some extensive bending of the written and unwritten rules is, therefore, commonplace in most social settings, and authorities, for a variety of reasons, do not fully enforce all the rules. An official who does attempt to enforce the letter of the law may upset everyone involved and everyone may push for his removal. Officials are, in fact, often hired on the basis of showing promise in their ability to bend the rules while maintaining good public relations with all parties.

The variety of alternatives to full-dress enforcement of regulations becomes the routine working practices of most officials.

The first alternative is simply to ignore the infractions. Most officials are aware of many infractions which they do nothing about. Often they will deliberately "not go looking" into things too closely as long as everything is going fairly well and the infractions occur quietly. If their "official attention" is called to the breeches they will be forced to take some kind of action. Channels for invoking this official attention often screen out all but the really serious cases.

Ignoring at least some kinds of violations is a necessary time-saving device. In most cases it would simply be impossible to deal with all infractions even if the authorities were single-mindedly bent on doing so. They must concentrate on maintaining order and on dealing with the more serious infractions, particularly those that disrupt the social processes and those that arouse attention from external publics. Most policemen, for example, ignore many violations in their precinct because there are more pressing, more serious crimes. *Many deviants have operated for years only because the authorities have been too busy to get around to them.*

Practical officials must be selective in enforcement and control. The rules are not regarded as equally important, even in strictly moral terms. Beyond such moral considerations, "seriousness" of violation is judged on the basis of ramifications for the internal workings of the milieu and the possible effects on relations between the milieu and its publics. Rules which have little consequence or which get in the way are not likely to be enforced with any consistency or vigor. So—in most social settings during most times—the largest number of rule-violations are just ignored.

Authorities may also punish infractions entirely informally and unofficially. In a "talking-to," the mildest and most common punishment, the official registers his disapproval, demands that the infractions be discontinued, points out the risks of continuing, and throws a scare into the culprit. This is the most likely course if the infraction is mild or if the infraction is a first known offense in an otherwise acceptable record. The higher the position and influence of the offender, the more likely this approach will be used.

For example, in a study of police handling of juvenile offenders, Piliavin and Briar found that Negroes and boys whose *appearance* fitted the delinquent stereotype were more frequently stopped and questioned by patrolmen and usually were treated more severely for the same violations than white "cleancut" youths. Less than fifteen percent of the "cooperative" violaters were arrested or officially cited while over ninety percent of the "uncooperative" ones received such severe treatment. Youths who were contrite, respectful, and fearful were perceived by patrolmen as "basically law-abiding or at least salvageable," but the offenders who were nonchalant, flippant, or antagonistic were defined as tough guys and punks who "fully deserved the most severe sanction: arrest."

The informal handling of a case depends upon several things outside the offense itself, the most notable of which is the status of the culprit. If the offender's position is relatively low in the milieu he is likely to get a straight ultimatum. If his or her position is high the reprimand will be more genteel and friendly. An official may take a conspiratorial tack with an influential violator, saying perhaps that he doesn't much care about the infraction but he's bound to register a complaint, "you understand." He may then urge the culprit to be more discrete or to desist for reasons of expediency. But if the violations of a high-prestige person come to the attention of external publics and become a scandal, they may receive more severe treatment than the more inconspicuous rank and file. A homosexual charge would probably hurt a U. S. Senator more than it would a nightwatchman.

Even with informal handling, however, some kind of record is likely to be made of the violation—at least the official will probably remember the incident—and this record may have subsequent consequences for the deviant. But the essential nature of informal action is that it bypasses official controls and thus will probably be invisible to the rest of the world.

A number of actions against violaters are more severe than informal reprimand but less severe than full official retribution. These usually involve some kind of formal censure, some punishment, and some form of probation. Authorities are usually given a good deal of discretion in choosing how to handle cases, and even when they don't have this discretion officially, they usually have it *de facto.* For example, judges have a variety of ways to reduce sentences (or increase them) even when the legal statutes clearly stipulate the sentence for particular crimes.

A special case of reducing penalties for infractions deserves separate discussion—the common situation where a district attorney, in collaboration with a suspect's court appointed lawyer, offers a "deal" where the suspect agrees to plead guilty to a lesser charge rather than go through a full trial for the more severe crime that provoked his arrest. David Sudnow found that over eighty percent of the cases in a west coast metropolitan district were settled out of court in such "deals." He found that this widespread practice had little to do with concern for the people arrested; indeed, *the public defenders usually agreed with the district attorney's office that the suspects were guilty and deserved punishment.* This practice guarantees a conviction while saving expense, effort, and the risk of losing the case (suspect found not guilty) if it went to trial.

Sudnow found that in the vast majority of cases the court-appointed lawyers acted essentially as co-workers with the prosecuting attorneys. They worked together to strike a balance where the culprit would "get his due" yet get something less than he might so that he would be willing to plead guilty.

The procedure works something like this. A youth might be arrested and thrown in jail for smoking marijuana or joyriding in a "borrowed" car. If he has no money, the court-appointed lawyer may come to him and say, "You're in real trouble, boy. I think they've got you cold and your conviction may get you a two-to-ten year sentence. If you plead guilty to 'being in a place where marijuana was used' or 'petty theft' I might be able to persuade the D.A. to accept the lesser charge and you'll probably get off with something light—six months in jail and a couple years probation. I'm not sure he'll go for it because he has an open and shut case against you, but it's worth a try." The realities of this half-typical situation are that even though the D.A. and P.D. routinely offer these reductions in exchange for a guilty plea the culprit may come off no better than if he had lost a full trial.

In the last decade or so, the alternative of referring culprits to counselling has become widespread. The violator is officially defined as confused or misguided or emotionally disturbed rather than bad or guilty. He is then referred to an agency specifically designed for handling such cases. Universities, the armed services, corporations and bureaus, high schools, and law enforcement organizations are employing this approach to an ever-increasing extent. This handling of deviants is most likely in cases of "crimes without victims," such as homosexuality, drug use, prostitution, and mental disturbance. There are no property damages, no "injured parties," and no coercions. Whatever the merits (and degradations) of the counselling treatment, this procedure saves the violator from full punishment and its long-term stigma.

This approach is certainly more liberal and humane than "an eye for an eye and a tooth for a tooth." The "treatment" may actually rehabilitate; compared to simple punishment, no doubt a greater number of people emerge as healthy individuals and useful citizens. But we mustn't gloss over its pitfalls. Such treatment is usually more custodial and punitive than publicly admitted, as many researchers have demonstrated. Delinquent retention centers and state mental hospitals, for example, serve largely to keep their "patients" under guard and away from society, often for an indeterminate time. A juvenile delinquent and a mental patient have fewer guaranteed rights than a prison convict and are more at the mercy of the staff. Also, as Erving Goffman and others have so well documented, such therapeutic procedures abound with personal degradations and flagrant invasions of privacy—the culprit is socially and psychologically naked before the voyeuristic gaze of the impersonal official and therapeutic community. If the culprit refuses to submit, he is marked as "uncooperative to treatment" and he soon discovers that submission to staff personnel is the price of "getting out." For a stark portrayal of these degradations read Erving Goffman's *Asylums* and Ken Kesey's *One Flew Over the Cuckoo's Nest*.

Even setting aside these underlying punishments and humiliations, many therapeutic and rehabilitative procedures are dubious. Powelson and Bendix, for example, found that prison psychiatry care amounts to little more than preaching an ultra-Puritan morality to inmates regarded as morally defective, and applying disciplinary measures, including denial of parole, to those who don't show enthusiastic agreement. Others, such as Kingsley Davis and C. Wright Mills, have asserted that the mental health professions are, despite their own claims, little more than discriminatory disseminators and enforcers of middle-class morality.

It must also be noted that boat-rocking juveniles or dependent relatives are sometimes dealt with by "railroading" them into ostensibly therapeutic commitments.

These are telling inadequacies and pitfalls in the therapeutic handling of rule-violators. But they are a gain over the straight punishment approach which prevailed until so recently. The danger is that such practices could become little more than compulsory thought reform *á la* Communist China and *1984*.

Another alternative employed with increasing frequency by the authorities is a *show* of full enforcement with a subsequent reduction of punishment. This is most common when the violation is serious, perhaps criminal, but the culprit is a first offender (in the eyes of the authorities) or of high rank. It is also the most common practice when the violation has attracted unfavorable attention from external publics or when the authorities are anxious to discourage similar infractions among the populace. The culprit is publicly and officially convicted, publicly labelled deviant, but then immediately put on probation or soon paroled. Slightly more than half (53%) of those convicted of crimes in 1965 were placed on probation instead of being sent to prison, and both probation and parole rates seem to be increasing. (Success rates for probation are about seventy-five percent.) A small proportion of convicted law-breakers actually serve out the full term of the sentences; even those convicted of murder stand a fairly good chance of being released on parole in seven to twenty years. The practice of releasing violators on probation is growing, partly because of the tremendous costs of imprisonment, but mainly because the realization seems to be growing in all quarters that prisons may breed more crime than they prevent and that it is better for the culprit and for society to rehabilitate and reintegrate the convict in the community.

These subsequent reductions are a quiet sequel to the public display of enforcement. For more serious deviations this approach has many attractions for officialdom: the public conviction serves simultaneously as a display of enforcement for the external publics and a warning example to the internal population, it demonstrates the competence of the officials, it punishes the culprit, and it is humane.

Probation and parole are not equally available to all convicted deviants, however. A host of studies has shown that racial and ethnic minorities, the lower classes, and those who are disreputable in the eyes of officialdom are more likely to be convicted, more likely to be severely sentenced, and less likely to get probation or parole than white Anglo-Saxon Protestants in good community standing. In a study of shoplifting, for instance, Mary Cameron found that "the likelihood of a Negro woman arrested in the store serving a jail sentence is about six times the likelihood of [a jail sentence for] a white woman," although the average value of the stolen merchandise was the same for the two groups. The literature on arrest, trial, and sentencing strongly suggests that the main variable determining outcomes of cases is the money the culprit has for good lawyers and appeals.

The standard working criteria used by officials in awarding suspended sentences, light sentences, or probation are simple and clearcut. The culprit's record and "character" are key factors in deciding whether the culprit is basically sound and just went a little wrong, is unstable but salvageable, or is a punk who deserves the heavy hand of the state. How contrite the person appears to be and how determined to "go straight" if given another chance are the chief ingredients in the judgment of character. Anyone who is recalcitrant or aggressive and anyone who insists on the moral legitimacy of what he's done in the face of the legal statutes can expect to serve time if he is convicted—it's that simple. A steady job, or the promise of one, and a stable place of residence with no aura of disreputability are main components of the person's record, along with previous arrests, grades, recommendations of officials who knew the culprit in the past. These factors are manipulated by skillful lawyers and the more sophisticated culprits, and they are summarized in the cynical convict adage: "Money talks and bullshit walks."

There is a growing reverse use of this official labelling with reduced punishment—the legal harassment of persons and groups such as hippies, campus protesters, peace demonstrators, and militant blacks who have fallen into disfavor with federal, state, and local Establishments. Long-haired youths, anti-war speakers, and restive blacks are arrested for minor offenses even when the arrest has slight legal grounds and is almost certain to be thrown out of court. In clashes with police, demonstrators are often taken on charges such as "disorderly conduct," "resisting arrest," or "assaulting an officer" although such resistance and assault may have consisted of no more than raising one's arms to protect one's head from swinging nightsticks. This approach seems to be becoming the main governmental strategy in the international youth-age conflict that now appears to be shaping up.

There's another type of reverse side of this approach that deserves mention. When a social setting is disrupted officialdom, to stop the trouble, will often grant amnesty to the leaders of the dissidents and pledge not to persecute them later. As the disputes are settled the leaders are, in perhaps the majority of cases, first let alone but punished when the authorities are firmly in control of things again. How people in general feel about this depends on whether they favor or oppose the dissidents, more than on the legality of the legal harassment.

If the violation is serious but not criminal, the deviant may simply be quietly dismissed. Often, innocuous reasons for the dismissal will be given so that neither the culprit nor the Establishment will be unduly embarrassed in public. Thus, again, the violation is punished with little or no scandal, the official has done his duty, and the culprit escapes the full force of the rules. Those offenders with high position and prestige in the milieu will usually be offered this course. Workmen are fired and enlisted men court martialed, but executives and officers are asked to resign.

The quiet dismissal is therefore most likely when the violation hasn't come to the attention of external publics and when the culprit is of high status. Indeed it seems to have always been true that one of the privileges of rank is to escape the full retribution of the society's reactions to deviance. This is a complex matter and there are exceptions, as, for instance, cases of discrimination against the privileged by proletarian officialdom. But even then, the wealth and connections of the privileged groups often enable many of them to escape.

The most extreme course if full and unequivocal labelling and punishment of the deviant. But this situation actually occurs rarely and almost always in a temporary "reign of terror" accompanying a change of officialdom or a cleanup campaign necessitated by pressures from external publics. When such stringent enforcement is launched by a particular official for no reason other than his own personal zeal, he is himself likely to be reprimanded by his superiors, subverted by some of his subordinates, and removed. That is, *an official must himself justify the full enforcement of the rules.* Full rule enforcement is seldom convenient to anyone. *Many deviants remain free and unmolested as a result.*

The more seasoned members of populations are aware of these alternatives to full enforcement of the rules, and they develop some skill in fabricating and dramatically presenting "their side" if they are caught. The fact that their side usually does have some validity and some extenuating circumstances provides further grounds for the official choosing a milder retribution. Culprits and officials thus frequently cooperate, at least tacitly, to arrive at a resolution of the violation which is somewhat satisfactory to all concerned—albeit the motives for this cooperation are not the same. Part of learning the ropes in any social setting is learning the "pitch" that stands the best chance of winning a reduced official reaction if you are caught at rule-breaking.

THE STRICTNESS OF THE RULES

The laws and unwritten rules which govern most social settings are therefore only sporadically and selectively enforced. But why are the rules so stringent if no one seriously intends to enforce them fully? Why aren't the rules changed to be more in line with the actual practices of the authorities?

In the first place many rules (like the Ten Commandments) are designed as ideals, as positive models toward which the population should strive, in addition to being negative limits. By making the rules more realistic the institution would hence lower the ideal standard of "good." Of course, few institutions live up to the ideals about how they should treat their populations. Most Americans sometimes violate the laws and, conversely, most American Establishments sometimes violate their Constitutions in dealing with their peoples.

Secondly, the strict rules are valuable as "public relations." They save the institution much criticism from external publics. In fact, many of these publics probably wouldn't accept changed rules which were more in line with the actual practices. For many reasons external publics usually demand strong controls over the population in question and having strict rules on the books is one means of placating them.

Third, and perhaps most important, the multitudes of stringent rules are very useful tools of the working official. When emergencies and changing conditions arise he has more freedom to maneuver than if the rules were true reflections of present practices. Strict rules can always be invoked if the official feels he needs them, and he comes off with the image of "a good guy" when he doesn't. The ironic height of this are the cases where concentration camp and chain gang prisoners have defined the camp commandant as a humane man and a secret sympathizer because he granted them a few amenities.

Since members of the population almost always stray beyond the rules, the actual boundaries of acceptable conduct can be drawn more narrowly with strict rules—even though they will diverge somewhat from the letter of these. If the coffee break limit is officially ten minutes, time off can realistically be held to perhaps twenty minutes; but if it were extended to twenty minutes, half an hour would be the realistic limit the authorities could impose.

Finally the factor of sheer historical inertia must be noted. Actually removing a rule from the books is far more difficult than just ignoring it because the procedures for revoking rules are usually quite complicated, and there is always the danger that some group will oppose such action. A government or organization that endures becomes overgrown with outdated rules.

Perhaps the main reason why many laws are not changed lies in the nature of politics. A good many officials will agree *in private* that our sex laws or our drug laws are grossly outdated, and the courts often show their own real views by throwing cases out of court or by giving light sentences. But these same officials and judges are seldom willing to risk their careers (appointed or elected) by taking strong public stands against such rules. A pot smoking lawyer told me, "Well, most of my clients get off with light sentences or probation." When asked, officials and professionals will sometimes say that they are working hard behind the scenes to bring about changes and that any public stand would jeopardize the slow progress being made. Meanwhile the laws remain and are sometimes enforced; people suffer heavy costs and perhaps serve a jail sentence for smoking a joint or going to bed with someone. I have been repeatedly told with regard to drug laws, sex laws, and abortion laws that the courts are waiting for the legislatures and the legislatures are waiting for the courts.

THE LINGERING OF TRACES

Whatever way officials choose to handle any particular violation, it may not be the end of the matter for the deviant. We saw in earlier chapters that becoming known as a deviant may have many far-reaching consequences. If any records of the violation exist, even only in the memories of the officials and other professionals having access to privileged information, the culprit's position in his environment suffers.

Even if no immediate reprisal is taken against the violator, he has a strike against him which:

A) Means he is likely to be treated more harshly for future violations.

B) Means he is subsequently vulnerable to retroactive reprisals. For instance, "boatrockers" are more likely to be replaced in a change of officialdom than the innocuous rank-and-file. Former culprits may find themselves assigned to more odious duties and passed over in promotions. For example, colleges around the country are now moving to establish procedures for denying scholarships and loans to students who participate in campus protests and demonstrations.

C) Means he must behave more conventionally henceforth. In game theory terms he must play to minimize losses rather than maximize gains. He is thus handicapped in competing against those who have a clean slate. He must forgo or be far more cautious about taking any gambles which even border on un-acceptability.

D) Means he is more explicitly "on probation" than his fellows who are not known to be rule-breakers.

In considering the effects of such lingering traces we must be careful not to overstate the case. For most people, these records may have few, if any, significant effects on their careers. The point is that they have the *potential* of having such effects and that this potential lingers beyond any official statute of limitations. Fears about such potential effects can also lead the person to change his behavior—in fear of retribution he administers a self-probation. Many people, of course, live and prosper in the face of a long string of such violations; but there are also many who have been ruined by them. Cogent examples of such retroactive punishments are the thousands of people whose careers suffered during the McCarthy era for having once been affiliated with some alleged communistic or socialistic organization, perhaps twenty years prior in their youth. So what happens in the long run to a person who has violated the prevailing standards of his society is dependent upon the shifts of history.

SEMI-OFFICIAL SOCIAL CONTROL

A wide variety of people, in addition to the authorities, some-times, semi-officially, helps regulate every population. These "semi-officials" are themselves essentially members of the population who partially and temporarily exercise some control. In their jobs they usually meet many people and often are better acquainted with the population than the officials. Hence they serve as "middlemen." Examples of semi-officials are landlords, teachers, bartenders, cab drivers, public utility employees, and, under extreme conditions, any full-fledged member of the population.

Semi-officials exercise some control directly, but their power is more tenuous and conditional than that of full-fledged officials. They are most effective in curbing the milder kinds of deviance through applying mildly negative sanctions—refusal to serve, a sharp glance, or verbal invectives like "quiet down." These milder sanctions are effective in the overwhelming majority of cases because the populace knows that the semi-official has direct "referral" power with authorities. That is, aside from their direct control powers (which range from verbal suggestion to eviction to the license to kill) semi-officials are empowered and under some obligation to refer gross offenders to the authorities. Such referrals are usually the last resort in their arsenal of controls, but the possibility lends force to their requests and reproofs.

Because the semi-official role is far more ambiguous than a full official role, its forcefulness depends to a much larger extent on the character of the person performing it. Deference is less automatic, an unconvincing display may be overridden by members of the populace, and the role may even be usurped by someone else.

A fairly large fraction of the populace will serve frequently or occasionally as semi-officials and they do much of the regulative work of the overtaxed authorities. Besides serving as enforcers, they serve as "listening posts" for the authorities. But their main function is to deal directly with the largest number of violations, particularly the milder violations of public peace and decorum. The daily problems of maintaining a minimum of public order and private discretion are left largely in their hands. In more serious disturbances semi-officials are also of crucial importance. Unlike the regular authorities, they are numerous and ubiquitous; therefore, they discover most deviants and are under obligation to inform their superiors. But since they are only partly official, they are only partly loyal, and seldom zealously inform. Indeed, they probably protect more deviants than they betray.

Social control within a setting is therefore something of a two-step process, with semi-officials mediating between the regular authorities and the populace on most occasions. The authorities hold semi-officials somewhat responsible and accountable for the populations under their purview and in this way motivate them to control, refer, and inform on the people—or at least make some show of doing so.

Semi-officials are perhaps even more likely than regular officials to selectively act. Their own values and prejudices enter into their handling of deviations and here is the first phase in the process of discriminatory enforcement we discussed earlier. Beyond this bias there is another bias shared with the full-fledged officials, a greater concern over those violations that disturb the peace. This sharing tends to produce a social quietus on the surface, which impels the populace to be clandestine. People learn early that it is often more important to be "cool" than to be "good."

The population in general is motivated to win the good graces of semi-officials because these mediators can grant favors and intercede with the authorities as well as punish. And like officials, semi-officials sometimes misuse their position to further their own personal ends. Since this role usually has some status, members may scramble to occupy it. For example, I have witnessed elaborate intrigues over who will become head dishwasher in a truck stop. Since the semi-official is in a good bargaining position he can favor or punish—the populace will court him. Waitresses flirt with the head waiter, students affably greet their professors, blacks go through the rituals of racial ettiquette with whites, and management trainees curry favor with executive secretaries.

Deviants are drawn to social settings where the semi-officials are permissive. And semi-officials who cater to deviant subcultures are often tolerated by the regular authorities because they keep deviant activities within bounds and act as informants when really serious violations occur. Most large and medium-sized cities have sections where this kind of arrangement is well-established.

Under special circumstances, it is expected that any full-fledged member of the social setting will step forward and act as a semi-official. For instance, in times of crisis, all citizens of a country are expected to act as deputies in behalf of their nation. And there is a tradition, older than recorded history, that the members of a tribe or community help one another in times of trouble. Ideally, all citizens will act semi-officially to curb and correct any deviations which may be dangerous to others or to the whole. In the ideal view, citizens will also act semi-officially to curb and correct any practices of the established officialdom that may be dangerous to others or to the whole. Needless to say, these traditions can provide the grounds for civil strife, as in our current generational rift where each camp claims to represent our social heritage, and each side calls the other deviant.

OUTCOMES

How do the actions of the authorities influence the long-term outcomes of deviant careers? And what becomes of the deviant in the end?

There is little doubt that time cures more deviants than any active social control program. The largest numbers of people experiment with deviant behavior off and on during certain periods of their lives, then eventually give it up. Deviant careers are more uncertain and abortive than conventional ones because there are almost always more problems and fewer stabilities and supports. As one respondent put it, in time even the full-fledged deviant usually "falls back exhausted into respectability." Most people, as they grow older, become more connected and involved in the major conventional institutions of their society; they have more legitimate opportunities open to them, and they risk more if they act upon illicit ones. Also their passion, their discontent, and their restlessness usually subside as their physiological vigor declines. Probably nothing stabilizes and conventionalizes as much as a steady job and a family.

There is even a good deal of evidence that as many people recover from mental illness through the simple passage of time as with any of our psychiatric therapies. This is whimsically called "the magic triangle" of the mentally disturbed—regardless of treatment one third are cured, one third improved, and one third unchanged.

Among long term deviants, the most common pattern is the establishing of a "double life" which attempts to include the best of both worlds. This usually entails some compartmentalization and schizophrenic splits, at least in the person's behavior if not in his head. And the double liver will usually experience a sort of mild, free-floating paranoia about discovery which never entirely disappears. Despite these costs and risks a good many people find this to be the most rewarding and self-expressive way of living.

There is a more curious outcome for many long term deviants. It is not uncommon for shifts in the prevailing climate of opinion around them to propel deviants back into the mainstream of society. The deviants don't change—the society around them does. Today's radical often becomes tomorrow's solid citizen as his once outlandish views become widely accepted. Likewise, today's sexual libertine may find, as the years pass, that the rest of society has caught up with him. And those in the current psychedelic generation are likely to be the squares whom today's infants will be rebelling against in twenty years.

Some deviants develop a way of life with few conventional ties or roles and they remain on the outskirts of society throughout their life-careers. Life on the fringes tends to be more harsh and uncertain and the number of people who pursue this course is much smaller than the number who lead a double-life or who sporadically dip into deviance. Despite the small and continually changing fringe population, there are well-established social and geographical "half-worlds," "night-worlds," "underworlds" for those who choose this way of life or are imprisoned in it.

The fewest yet best known deviants are chronic offenders or mental patients who may spend most of their adult lives in various prisons or hospitals. These are the double-failures, unable to make it in either conventional or deviant society.

There's no doubt that officials have some success in keeping deviance within bounds. Marijuana use and abortions, for instance, would certainly be even more widespread than they now are if it weren't for the work of the authorities. In this way they do somewhat preserve the status quo of our society. But what overall influence do they have upon deviants themselves?

Everything taken together, I strongly suspect that officials now further alienate more culprits than they recruit back into conventional society, and I think they imprison at least as many people in deviance as they rehabilitate. We must remember that, with a sprinkling of exceptions, officials come from, are hired by, and belong to the dominant majority. It is not surprising that they focus their efforts on maintaining and perpetuating their social order rather than on accomodating and correcting deviants. In this fundamental sense, even "liberal" officials are basically conservative.

CHAPTER NINE

HIDDEN

COSTS

A society could, theoretically, have a wide range of postures toward deviations within its ranks, varying from complete suppression to complete permissiveness. Each of these postures would entail certain "costs" as well as certain "returns" for the society. The costs and returns of many of these approaches to deviance must be speculative, however, because they have never been tried. Necessities of survival and the understandable wish of the privileged groups to maintain the status quo have united to make *all societies repress deviance.* At times permissiveness has reigned by default, when a social order disintegrated to the point that most persons and small groups were on their own. But the license to "do your own thing" has never been granted the members of any stable society. Even when there was no tyranny of the officialdom, the tyranny of tradition has kept most of the populace in check. The idea of mass permissiveness has never been seriously considered by anyone but a small minority of intellectuals and a few fringe groups.

Today it looks like this state of affairs may be changing. Restrictiveness versus permissiveness has become something of a national debate and more and more concrete issues such as student politics, sexual freedom, psychedelic drugs, and the draft are being hotly argued in terms of permissiveness. Many favor restriction because they fear that a wave of anarchy threatens the very fabric of our society. Conversely, many other people argue for increased permissiveness as fulfillment of the long-held humanistic dream of individual freedom and self-determination. There is also a growing belief that suppression does more harm than good to society as well as to the culprits. And beyond these issues, our minorities, many young people, and numbers of prominent opposition intellectuals are coming more and more to accuse officials of misusing their offices—of employing repression to perpetuate a society that benefits their own groups at the expense of others.

So suppression versus tolerance is both an issue in its own right and a focal point for other internal conflicts. Since our only experience has been with varying degrees of suppression, its costs are more definite than our speculations about permissiveness.

THE HIDDEN COSTS OF SUPPRESSION

My major assertion, backed by a growing volume of literature, is that the alienation, psychological conflict, and antisocial behavior of deviants stem largely from society's suppressive attitude and treatment of deviance—not from anything necessarily inherent in the deviance itself. To put this another way, society's attempts to suppress deviations are unfortunate for the society as well as the deviant. The costs to society can outweigh the benefits.

Ostracism and suppression of the deviant no doubt help reduce deviance; but when the rejection is internalized by those who do deviate it creates self-condemnation and other psychological problems. Probably no deviants are impervious to the slings and arrows of an outraged society. And since the deviant is well aware that conventional society abhors him, he is very likely to reciprocate by becoming alienated from the society. No doubt many outsiders and rebels have been created by the continued enforcement of our current marijuana laws. It gives one pause to think that millions of Americans now stiffen guiltily and perhaps angrily when they see a police car go by.

Strong public antipathy produces in the deviant a reverberating negativism toward society. Such negativism in turn only serves to confirm the public's original antipathies, and, as society takes further suppressive action, the deviant becomes more estranged and embittered toward his parent culture. For example, the hippie movement began as a fringe development that was quite mild even in its legal violations, but through the process just described there are now uneasy areas where armed police face armed dissidents. This process also transforms many a group of teenage boys into a "delinquent gang."

Part of the problem is that our society, as most others, provides few "reentry" routes back from deviance. We have succeeded in getting past the days when a girl who has been "touched" outside of marriage is forever a fallen woman, and we don't go entirely on the philosophy that crime and mental disturbance signify incurable taint. But the deviant is still typically isolated, considered less than human, discriminated against, and hounded by his past record. Many deviants would reenter conventional society if they could, but the obstacles are too great. Aside from humane considerations this means that a large proportion of deviants are not only lost as contributing members of society but become prodigious public expenses. We produce our own rebels.

When human desires are blocked and repressed by social taboos another problem is created. The repressed desires, be they sexual cravings or aggressive feelings or a longing for respect and material goods, don't just evaporate. They erupt later—but in a more antisocial form, less under the person's or the society's control. In looking for disturbed children psychiatrists are learning to pass over the rowdy youth (with a word of reassurance for the teacher or parent) and give their attention to the "model child" who sits quietly and does everything he's told. By taking a strong suppressive position, a society practically guarantees that whatever deviance does occur will be compounded with antisocial feelings—robbers brutally beat their victums, rapists slash the women to pieces, and embittered demonstrators set fires and shoot policemen.

It must be remembered that the vast bulk of deviance need not involve any coercion or infringement of others' rights. Most deviance is either strictly personal or the cooperative action of willing partners. The violence and crimes against others almost always stem from the cycle of mutual antagonisms between a punitive society and its antagonized deviants. Violence is not inherent in the deviance itself, and under more permissive conditions does not occur.

When certain behaviors are made illegal and strongly suppressed, they are automatically put beyond the reach of any effective supervision or regulation. The outlawing of the labor movement in Europe during the last century is a dramatic example of what can happen as a result. Under such harsh repression the originally quite humanistic labor movement evolved into the far more extreme and revolutionary Communist movement which has now succeeded in gaining control of half the world. It is almost a historical law that repressive Establishments breed brutalized revolutionaries and that in the ensuing conflicts everybody loses. Early Christianity had a similar revolutionary character that faded only when it became the official state religion of the late Roman Empire.

But there are side-effects of suppression that pervade society at an even more concrete level. When certain popular behaviors are outlawed, a powerful, illicit "underworld" develops to service the deviants. Such illegal networks will arise simply because of profits. The fact is that crime does pay, sometimes quite handsomely. The average professional criminal probably makes more money, works less, and runs no more risks than the legitimate business entrepreneur.

Illicit organizations are thus indirectly created and subsidized by laws against deviance. For example, the Prohibition Era has largely provided the tax-free capital for the many and diverse activities of present-day organized crime in America—profits that were plowed back into narcotics, gambling, prostitution, and political corruption. The fact that such illegal networks don't pay taxes is probably the least of the problems created. The extra-legal organizations are interested in recruiting new customers for their goods and services for exactly the same reasons that conventional businessmen want to increase their volume of sales. To the extent that their "sales promotion" is successful, deviance rates may actually rise.

Services are more expensive when illicit, which produces "secondary crimes." Perhaps the best examples are the stealing, prostitution, drug-peddling, and so on that heroin addicts frequently resort to as their only means of paying the incredibly high price of their narcotic on the black market. Suppression thus has the side-effect of increasing the incidence of other types of crime and deviance.

In contrast to the American strategy of harsh suppression, the British have dealt with narcotics use by providing virtually free drugs to all registered addicts. Edwin Schur and others have documented the three main effects of this strategy: 1) black market drug syndicates can't make money so they wither away; 2) addicts needn't resort to other crimes to pay for drugs, and their crime rates are the same or lower than that of the general population; 3) neither addicts nor drug merchants are motivated to get more people hooked so there has been no appreciable increase in addiction rates.

Even if a person doesn't resort to secondary crimes to pay for illicit goods and services, he very likely will deny himself and his family such things as food, shelter, and adequate medical care. Since illicit services are almost always more expensive than the same services when they are legitimate, this drain upon the population's resources must be counted as another hidden cost of suppression.

Also the quality of the illegal goods and services is often shoddy and sometimes extremely dangerous. During Prohibition many people died drinking "bathtub gin"; veneral disease is spread by prostitutes not required to have regular medical examinations; thousands of girls have been injured or killed by incompetent abortionists (whereas legal abortions performed by competent doctors in modern hospitals are safe and simple); untold numbers of people have been harmed by impure black market narcotics and psychedelic drugs, and so on and so on. If you feel that any teenager who buys black market LSD deserves to be bum-tripped by its impurities or that any girl who gets involved in a clandestine sexual escapade deserves to be mained for life by a coat-hanger abortionist, then I suggest you look into a mirror and reflect on your own depravities.

Other hidden costs are more intangible than tax losses or the alienation of culprits but are perhaps the heaviest price of suppression. From a broader perspective, harsh suppression of deviance usually boils down to a tyranny of the majority over the minorities of a country. In the United States the life-style and even the prevailing vices of the effective majority WASPS (White Anglo-Saxon Protestants) group are permitted while some aspects of the life-style and most "vices" of minorities are ruthlessly outlawed. For example, marijuana, the favored intoxicant of today's youth, is outlawed while liquor, the favored intoxicant of adults, is promoted with all the wiles of American advertising.

An enriched and flexible culture almost has to permit the flowering of minority and fringe life-styles as well as the prevailing majority ones. The alternative is the straitjacketing of thought and deed and the alienation of whole segments of the populace. Under these conditions everyone fears to be even a little different or a little daring and as a result everyone's life is stunted. And no one is very much free. Optimism and playfulness are very likely to be replaced with free floating paranoia.

A society that doesn't tolerate much deviation curbs divergence of all kinds, including creativity. The threat of being labelled heretic locks the population into a rigid and ritualistic way of life where nothing is ventured and nothing is gained. Such societies cannot change with changing conditions—they can only fall apart. Alfred North Whitehead, Erich Fromm and others have pointed out that this kind of fossilization and shattering is the fate of most societies and it could be the fate of our own.

The final, most telling argument against strict suppression of deviance is that it doesn't work. It fails to curb most forms of deviance under most conditions. In fact the main function of suppression is to provide emotional satisfaction to the suppressors themselves. As Emile Durkheim pointed out long ago, deviants serve as a scapegoat for some of the unresolved frustrations and aggressions of the public through the same processes that underlie discrimination against racial and ethnic minorities. Since the source of the original frustrations and aggressions is not the scapegoat, the psychological relief is only temporary. But there are always more deviants and ethnic minorities.

Whatever psychological functions suppression serves for the public and its officialdom, it fails almost completely in most cases as a deterrent. The main result of Prohibition was the growth of organized crime in America; although laws against marijuana use have never been stiffer, use has never been greater and is now increasing at an epidemic rate; harsh treatment of campus protestors has only further radicalized the entire youth subculture; and the handling of social problems that produce mental disturbance by merely isolating and tranquilizing those who show up as the most obvious casualties has done nothing to reduce stress and anxiety in our environment.

THE COSTS OF PERMISSIVENESS

Everything that was said in the last section would suggest that permissiveness is the only sensible approach with deviance. But permissiveness has its costs too.

A main problem is that some people will take advantage of a permissive situation to do things which those who gave the permission won't like. A beautiful example of this irony can be seen in the generational conflicts so prevalent today. Many liberal parents raised their children to make up their own minds and find their own paths. And now their youthful offspring won't obey them or agree with them.

Of course if permissiveness exists only in the sense that "you can do what you want as long as you obey us" it isn't permissiveness at all. True permissiveness does inevitably entail the risk that others will not do what we approve and we must be able to stand it when this occurs or we can't afford to be tolerant.

Historically, only the privileged classes and the ruling elites have lived in anything like a permissive environment. From the age of the Pharaohs on down to our own present society, those in power have used their positions largely to perpetuate and enhance their own advantages through coercing and manipulating the rest of the populace. There have been notable exceptions—men who have used their permissive positions for the benefit of all—but these cases are notable exactly because they are exceptions. Even professional groups, like the medical profession, have nearly always taken advantage of whatever power and influence they could muster to make themselves more comfortable and further their own self-interests. Our own leaders and professionals having abused the permissiveness that goes along with their positions, there is every reason to believe that the rest of the population might seek its own betterment if given the chance. A more emancipated populace seeking *its* comfort and self-interest would probably generate many social upheavals and might well mark the end of the present status quo. This upheaval might still be preferable to violent revolution where everybody usually loses, but the groups in power have always been notoriously short-sighted along these lines.

More permissiveness would probably also mean that deviants would no longer be societal scapegoats. We would have to face our inadequacies and social failings directly, which would no doubt be traumatic at first but eventually more profitable than continuing to use the deviant as the outlet of our unresolved frustrations and hostilities.

Recognizing the dangers inherent in such unbridled freedom of thought and behavior, the Russians and Chinese have simply outlawed it, while the United States and other Western nations have remained indecisive on the issue, although our current political backlashes and squarelashes may signify a trend.

Real permissiveness toward deviance, or any great divergence in attitudes and actions, would require an openness of mind and a willingness to risk change.

CHAPTER TEN

DEVIANT

FUTURES

The myth of peculiar, alien deviants, of *thems* that we can cull out, label, and deal with, continues to mislead both authorities and laymen. The whole area of deviance actually boils down to: 1) inter-group power struggles where the winners make their own standards the law for all, 2) flaws and inadequacies in the society which force some of the population to seek expression and fulfillment on the fringes, 3) the feedback from harsh public treatment, official and informal, of the deviant. Most deviants at any one time are "tourists on the fringe" and what is peculiar about them is their minority position.

One of the conclusions from my study of deviance is that every deviant subculture that develops is reflecting an ill or inadequacy in the social fabric itself. Its contents are the clues as to how that society is failing to meet the needs and wants of its people. For example, sexual deviants graphically point up the various deep-rooted sexual hangups of our society. In similar fashion, the Black Panthers signify our racial inequalities and where they can lead. Psychedelic drug users may be a reminder of how confining and "soulless" our overly rational and materialistic way of life may have become. Delinquent gangs demonstrate how we have failed to provide anything like an adequate urban environment for growing up in. The growth of radicalism on the far Left and the far Right may be a good barometer of how our present social and political system engenders widespread feelings of frustration and impotence and alienation. School dropouts and growing truancy rates may best be understood as indictments of the schools and the teachers. And our widespread mental illness must say something about the health and vigor of our major institutions. Society can try to change the conditions giving rise to these "deviant subcultures." Or it can tolerate its deviant fringes. Or it can try to suppress them and wait for the explosion.

There will probably come a day when the widespread breaking of any rule or informal convention will be a signal which automatically starts not a hunt for a culprit but an investigation to determine the cause and the mending of the tear in the social fabric. A fringe might be tolerated or even encouraged to accomodate the wide divergencies of belief and behavior proven characteristic of humans. I suspect that this will prove to be the only effective way of handling "the deviance problem."

As long as a society fails to satisfy the desires of its members, we can expect deviance. The forms of deviance will change as societies change in what they allow and what they forbid, what they provide and what they fail to provide. It's hard to conceive of any present society which would be able or willing to encompass and contain the whole spectrum of its population's views and behaviors.

People will only stay within the law, in the last analysis, when they are satisfied in doing so. And since this is not happening there will be some people who will follow the path expressed in a line from the current music scene: "I'll go Outside where darkness sets me free."